# CONTEMPORARY ENGLISH
## LITERACY

Janet Podnecky

CONTEMPORARY BOOKS

*a division of* NTC/CONTEMPORARY PUBLISHING GROUP
Lincolnwood, Illinois USA

Cover Illustration: Regan Dunnick

Interior Illustrations: David Will, Adam Young

ISBN: 0-8092-0697-8

Published by Contemporary Books,
a division of NTC/Contemporary Publishing Group, Inc.
© 1999 NTC/Contemporary Publishing Group, Inc.,
4255 West Touhy Avenue, Lincolnwood (Chicago), Illinois 60646-1975 U.S.A.
All rights reserved. No part of this book may be reproduced, stored in a retrieval system, or
transmitted in any form or by any means, electronic, mechanical, photocopying, recording,
or otherwise, without prior permission of NTC/Contemporary Publishing Group, Inc.
Manufactured in the United States of America.

9 0 VL 0 9 8 7 6 5 4 3 2 1

# Contents

# Scope and Sequence: Literacy

| Unit | Topic | Culture Focus | Literacy Skills | Functions | SCANS Competencies |
|------|-------|---------------|-----------------|-----------|--------------------|
| Unit A | Preliteracy | | Shape recognition, directionality, recognizing, tracing, copying uppercase letters | | Foundation Skills |
| Unit B | Preliteracy | | Shape recognition, directionality, recognizing, tracing, and copying lowercase letters; matching uppercase and lowercase letters; numbers 1–10 | | Foundation Skills |
| 1 | Human Relations: Greetings | Greetings at school and work | Interpreting and identifying ideographs signifying male and female; sight word recognition | Greetings; stating one's name | Foundation Skills |
| 2 | Numbers | Counting | Recognizing, tracing, and copying numbers; matching numbers and quantities; understanding numbers 1–20 | Repeating words for clarification | Foundation Skills |
| 3 | Home and Neighborhood: Home | Filling out forms | Understanding simple street addresses; identifying name, city, and address on a simple form; matching words and pictures; copying and writing phone numbers and addresses | Identifying; requesting information | Foundation Skills |
| 4 | Transportation and Travel: Directions | Getting to know your town | Understanding simple directions and spatial orientation; sight word recognition; matching numbers and quantities; identifying room numbers and sequence on a simple diagram; understanding numbers 21–30 | Identifying; asking for clarification; requesting information | Foundation Skills |
| 5 | People and Machines: Time | U.S. attitudes toward time | Understanding time and reading clocks; reading signs with business hours indicated; reading analog clocks; understanding numbers 31–60 | Showing gratitude; telling time | Foundation Skills |
| 6 | Home and Neighborhood: Family | Sharing family information | Understanding words for family members; identifying family members and talking about family; reading simple biographical information forms; copying personal information onto a simple form; numbers in the tens, from 10 to 100 | Identifying; demonstrating | Foundation Skills |
| 7 | Employment and Opportunity: Jobs | Mini-résumés | Understanding job titles; identifying job titles, times, and phone numbers in simple job ads; sight word recognition; reading the year in figures; recognition of work signs | Expressing state of being | Foundation Skills |
| 8 | Consumer Economics: Money | Shopping | Reading prices and price tags; reading symbols for dollars and cents; identifying amounts on coins and paper money; relating prices to coins and bills; adding and subtracting amounts of money | Requesting information; expressing gratitude | Foundation Skills |
| 9 | Healthy Living: Food | Groceries | Identifying food items; reading names of food items; reading labels and ads for food; writing prices | Requesting information; giving information | Foundation Skills |

# Introduction

## Program Components and Philosophy

*Contemporary English* is a five-level interactive topic-based English-as-a-Second-Language series for adult learners ranging from the beginning-literacy level to the high-intermediate level. The series includes

- Student Books for classroom use
- Workbooks for independent use at home, in the classroom, or in a lab
- Audiocassettes for individual student, classroom, or lab use and
- Teacher's Manuals, with reproducible activity masters and unit progress checks for assessment. These materials were correlated from inception to the California Model Standards for Adult ESL Programs, the MELT Student Performance Levels, and the SCANS (Secretary's Commission on Achieving Necessary Skills) Competencies.

Unique among adult ESL series, *Contemporary English* presents high-interest topics as a framework for developing a wide variety of language, thinking, and life skills. In addition to focusing on listening, speaking, reading, and writing skills, *Contemporary English* integrates work on language structures; problem-solving, critical-thinking, and graphic-literacy skills; and—increasingly important—work-related skills.

*Contemporary English* empowers students to take charge of their learning and to develop strong communication skills for the real world. For example, each unit in Books 1–4 falls under one of the following broad topics: Home and Neighborhood, People and Machines, Employment and Opportunity, Human Relations, Consumer Economics, Community Services, Transportation and Travel, Healthy Living, History and Geography, and Arts and Entertainment. (The lowest-level book, *Contemporary English* Literacy, addresses all of these topics except History and Geography and Arts and Entertainment.) In short, the series addresses topics of interest and concern to adult learners.

*Contemporary English* presents engaging and meaningful situations that provide a context for grammar structures, listening activities, and an emphasis on the world of work. Within this framework each unit offers a wealth of pair and group activities, often with designated team roles, and frequent individual and group presentations to the class. This approach mirrors the team organization characteristic of today's workplace and reflects the recent influence on education of the Department of Labor's SCANS report.

## Teaching Suggestions

In general, keep the following suggestions in mind when you introduce activities from this series.

1. Rather than direct the classroom, try to manage or facilitate learning and encourage your learners to take active roles, even at the lowest levels of instruction.

2. Model activities before learners do them so that learners have a clear idea of how to work with a partner or a group.

3. Whenever possible, use students or classroom objects and people in your models. For example, say, "I am a teacher" or "She is a student." Move around the class and use gestures to convey meaning.

4. Review the directions orally and ask learners if they have questions.

5. Monitor learners as they do the activities.

6. Provide follow-up activities in some of these ways:
   - When appropriate, post learners' work on the classroom walls for them to read.
   - Have pairs or small groups share role-played conversations with the rest of the class.
   - From time to time, have learners informally reflect on their participation by asking themselves questions such as these: "How well did I understand the activity? Was I a good listener? How much did I participate?"

As you progress through the units, always try to consider the book as a meaningful whole. Whenever possible, review aspects of content, language, vocabulary, and workplace skills, and incorporate them into each new unit. In this way, the process of recycling—a strong feature of this series—can be customized to meet the needs of your class.

General extension activities can be used in all units. In Book 1 you can use TPR (Total Physical Response) activities quite successfully as extension. True role-playing can be used especially from Book 2 on up. Improvisation can be used in Books 3 and 4. Strip stories can be created from the readings at all levels. Higher-level students can be asked to read or find newspaper and magazine articles related to unit topics. And for classrooms or programs with technological capability, the Internet, word-processing, database, and even spreadsheet activities related to series topics—such as job-search and citizenship issues—can be highly motivating and also practical, as students can list this experience for employers in their job-skills summary.

Use of monolingual English dictionaries is appropriate in Books 3 and 4, and bilingual native-language dictionaries can be used at all levels.

## Dictations

You may want to do a dictation activity every time the class meets. Dictation is a good way to practice several English skills simultaneously, as learners listen, write, and read sentences in English. You can choose two sentences from one of the Scenes or a short section from one of the readings. Follow these steps.

1. Tell learners to listen to the first sentence but not write it.

2. Repeat the sentence. Tell learners how many words are in it.

3. Give learners time to write the sentence.

4. Repeat the sentence again if needed.

5. Show learners where to find the sentence in the book.

## Language Experience Stories

At the lower levels of the series, you may also want to use learner-generated language experience stories in your teaching approach. If you are not yet comfortable using language experience stories as a whole-class activity, the following steps may be helpful:

1. Ask the class to look at a photo or illustration related to the content of the unit.

2. Have learners talk about the visual.

3. Write what they say.

4. Read their words to them.

5. Ask if they want to make any changes or corrections, but keep the emphasis on the connection between spoken and written language, not on correct grammar.

6. Read the story aloud while learners follow along.

7. Point to words and sentences and have learners read them to you.

8. Have learners practice reading the story as many times as they show interest in doing so.

## Journal Writing

You may want to have higher-level students keep journals to improve their written English. If you have not monitored journal writing before, try following these suggestions:

1. Give learners a formal or informal schedule on which you will review the journals.

2. Tell them to write about anything they are interested in learning about that day or week. Low-level students or those who have little practice writing may need to write just one sentence every day at the end of class.

3. After reading each journal, write several sentences or questions about the entries.

4. Don't make corrections unless the individual learner asks you to do so.

5. Discuss journal entries with their student authors.

## Bringing the World to the Classroom

1. Ask learners to look in magazines or newspapers for stories related to the unit. An alternative is to bring periodicals to class yourself and look through them together.

2. Listen to the radio or television for stories about topics related to those in the units. Ask learners if they have heard or seen the stories.

3. Talk about the stories in class and relate them to the unit.

Always encourage learners to take active roles, even at the lowest levels of instruction. One way in which you can move learning in a more active direction is to have students ask the questions provided in the unit-specific notes in this Teacher's Manual. You can write the questions on 3 x 5 inch index cards, hand them to students, and let them direct their own and one another's learning. Higher-level students can add a question of their own to the cards, and students can exchange cards. The possibilities for encouraging active learning with *Contemporary English* are unlimited.

## Graphic Organizers

These useful tools for organizing individual or collective thinking and writing play a central role in *Contemporary English*. Graphic organizers such as Venn diagrams, idea maps, T-charts, and Johari windows can be used successfully in the learning process. Graphic organizers are particularly helpful in developing higher-level thinking skills, and the visual aspect of these tools makes them ideal for visual learners.

Even among experienced teachers and teacher trainers, there is surprising variation among terms used to identify certain procedures and techniques for language learning, so the following definitions may be useful to you in working with graphic organizers. Although you may already be familiar with the definitions, consider presenting them to your class and explaining that you will be using certain organizers throughout the term. In the student materials themselves, efforts have been made to provide very brief definitions in context so that students will feel comfortable with the designated organizers for their level even when working independently.

**Johari window.** A square divided into four parts; a four-paned window. While Joharis can, of course, compare four different things, they are most commonly used to compare and contrast two things in this way:

panel 1: A has/does/etc. this

panel 2: B has/does/etc. this

panel 3: Both A and B have/do/etc. this

panel 4: Neither A nor B has/does/etc. this

**T-chart.** A two-column chart (in the form of a T), used to compare or contrast.

**Venn diagram.** Two overlapping circles, also used to compare and contrast. Properties of two things or concepts are written in the outer portions of the circles. In the overlapping section, shared properties are written.

**Idea map.** An organizer used to brainstorm ideas and gather information. The map has a central circle with a topic word, phrase, or sentence and connected circles surrounding it in which related or subordinate ideas or examples are written.

**Time line.** Even at the lowest levels of English instruction, the time line is a useful tool for teaching sequencing skills. As your students do the time line activities related to the content of their books and workbooks, you can guide them, whenever appropriate, to create their own time lines for different stages of their lives. This process involves gathering data and subsequently organizing it and presenting it to an audience.

## The Student Book

Before you begin the first **Scene,** discuss—or explain with words and gestures if necessary—the meaning of the title, which can be a springboard to understanding the central issues. You also may wish to bring in photos, illustrations, and/or realia that illustrate the content and the concept. At more advanced levels, ask students themselves to predict what the unit is going to be about.

Ask questions that encourage students to contribute general information and personal information related to the topic (for example, "Fatima, do many people have big families in your country? Juan, do you have brothers?").

Write some of the questions and answers on the board or provide a handout.

You may wish to have students ask and answer some of the same questions in pairs.

## Scenes

Each unit is divided into two parts, each of which begins with a **Scene** that presents, in comic-strip format, incidents from the lives of newcomers to the United States or aspects of U.S. culture that students encounter regularly. Lively, humorous, and dramatic, the **Scenes** engage students in the unit topics—usually by presenting typical problems in the lives of average people. A series of discussion questions proceeds from factual comprehension of the **Scene** to personalization and, in Books 3 and 4, problem solving. For example, at the highest level the sequence is *Facts* (comprehension questions), *Feelings* (inference), *And You?* (application), *Comparisons* (often between the students' native countries and the United States), and, finally, the *Action* problem-solving questions—for example, *What should ___ do?*

Here are some techniques to enhance class work for each **Scene** with lower-level learners:

1. Write the conversation on the board.

2. Read or play each line of the conversation twice and ask the class to repeat it. Whenever possible, emphasize a holistic approach. In other words, try to have learners deal with whole chunks of language, rather than breaking language down word by word.

3. Read the language that learners have difficulty pronouncing and ask them to repeat words and phrases as a class as often as necessary. As soon as pronunciation improves, work with repetition of the entire line again.

4. Ask individual students to repeat the line.

5. Have students do a final choral repetition. Then move to the next line.

6. As each new line is practiced, add it to the previously learned section of the Scene. Continue this way until students can repeat the entire dialogue. At higher levels you may wish to have learners read the cartoon in groups of twos or threes.

7. Review new or difficult vocabulary.

8. Say the words and have learners repeat them.

9. Elicit definitions of the words. Check comprehension. If students cannot define the words, you can provide definitions or examples.

10 Extend the **Scene** by doing some or all of the following activities:

- Have learners spell the words (on the board or aloud).

- Use the words in two or three sentences.

- Ask learners to use the words in sentences.

- Have students practice in pairs as you move around the classroom, checking pronunciation.

- Have learners take roles and read the dialogue aloud. Allow several pairs or groups of students to present each **Scene** for the class.

- Have partners take turns dictating the conversations. Student A can dictate while Student B writes the conversation in his or her ESL notebook.

- Write three to five sentences on small paper strips and hand these to individual learners. When prompted, each learner can read his or her sentence. You can then write each on the board or on an overhead transparency. Lower-level classes can copy the sentences. The class can then order the sentences chronologically by assigning a number to each one.

- Read a summary of the **Scene.** Then write it on the board or an overhead transparency, or provide it on a handout. Remove the summary and have learners write their own.

- After learners answer the questions under the **Scene**, have each one write one or two additional questions to ask other learners.

- Have students retell the story and write about the pictures in their own words.

These activities are particularly useful with multilevel classes. The **Scenes** introduce students to the topic of the unit, give them a context for the grammar, get them interested and involved in the story, and build a context for the unit.

## Sound Bites

After each opening **Scene** comes **Sound Bites,** a focused listening task that includes prelistening and postlistening work. **Sound Bites** presents target content and language structures through lively conversations and other samples of natural speech, such as telephone answering-machine messages and transportation announcements.

For any **Sound Bites** activity, you can follow these steps:

1. Read the directions aloud.
2. Model the directions.
3. Tell students what kind of conversations or passages they will listen to.
4. Read or play the tape for each individual **Sound Bites** item several times. Speak at a normal speed. Remember that learners don't need to understand every word to get meaning.
5. Model the appropriate written response.
6. Let students listen as often as they want.

At lower levels let students direct their learning by frequently asking them questions such as "Do you need to listen again?" and teaching them to ask clarification questions such as "Can you repeat number six?" At higher levels you may wish to have students take notes as they listen.

You can provide repeated active-listening experiences for all levels of students by assigning a different focus for each one. For example, play **Sound Bites** the first time and ask students, "Have you heard anything like this before? Where were you?" Then play the tape again and have students listen for vocabulary. A third time they can listen for something else—perhaps to complete the task or to listen for specific questions you provide, such as "What kind of person is Jerry?" Encourage students to compare answers. As an extension activity, later in the unit, you may wish to make the **Sound Bites** into a cloze exercise, for example, by leaving out the examples of the grammar point throughout.

## Vocabulary Prompts, Your Turn, and In Your Experience

**Vocabulary Prompts, Your Turn,** and **In Your Experience** occur within the units at the point of need, rather than in a fixed or unvarying part of each unit. **Vocabulary Prompts,** for example, serves to isolate challenging vocabulary before a listening or reading task. **Your Turn,** a follow-up to reading, listening, or structure practice, serves as a participatory task. **In Your Experience,** an activity drawing on students' prior knowledge and personal lives, allows learners to personalize the topics and relate them to their own experience.

In Book 1, before students actually open their books to one of these vocabulary sections, you may want to prepare them by doing the following:

1. Show related pictures, maps, and realia.
2. Provide clear pronunciation models and ask students to repeat each word or term several times.
3. Provide additional explanations and examples as needed and use people and objects in the classroom whenever possible.
4. Finally, preview the **Sound Bites** tape and ask learners to listen for the words in the **Vocabulary Prompts** box.

A way to maximize learners' opportunities to practice oral communication in the **Your Turn** and **In Your Experience** sections is to use three-way interviews. These proceed in the following way: Students 1 and 2 talk to each other; Students 3 and 4 talk to each other. Then 1 and 3 talk, and 2 and 4 talk. Finally, 1 and 4 talk, and 2 and 3 talk. You can then assign all students with one number to report their results to the class. This procedure allows everybody plenty of opportunities to talk.

# Spotlight

Throughout *Contemporary English*, grammar structures are first contextualized in the **Scenes** and listening activities, and then presented, practiced, and applied on follow-up **Spotlight** pages. Appearing two to four times in each unit, the **Spotlight** pages model target structures in contexts related to the unit topic. Special **Spotlight** feature boxes present the target structures schematically and provide brief, straightforward explanations when necessary. Exercises following the structure presentations allow students to manipulate the structures in meaningful contexts, such as stories or real-life situations. **Spotlight** pages usually end with a **Your Turn** and/or an **In Your Experience** activity providing communicative application of the new structures.

To present the **Spotlight** structures most effectively to learners using Books 1 and 2 of the series, try the following sequence of steps:

1. Ask questions that either lead into the target structures or contain the target structures. For example, to lead into the target structures, you can ask questions that would normally take an answer with the target structure. You can then elicit the correct structure or, if students are unable to produce it, provide a sentence containing the structure. In this way, you will establish an appropriate context for the target structure from the beginning.

2. Guide students through the language forms in the **Spotlight** box.

3. Elicit and answer any questions learners may have.

4. Provide oral practice for correct pronunciation of the sentences containing the forms.

5. Read any rules that follow the example sentences, and then return to the sentences to demonstrate those rules.

With learners using Books 3 and 4, the following suggestions may help:

1. Ask questions that either lead into the target structures or contain the target structures. For example, to lead into the target structures, you can ask questions that would normally take an answer with the target structure. You can then elicit the correct structure or, if students are unable to produce it, provide a sentence containing the structure. In this way, you will establish an appropriate context for the target structure from the beginning.

2. After you have elicited or provided several examples of the target structure, try to elicit rules from learners. Many may have encountered the structures before or may actually have studied them formally.

3. You may wish to put sentences on the board for students to complete with the target structures. You can continue in this way until the class begins to get a feeling for the new structure.

4. Draw two faces. Write a conversation in speech bubbles for them but leave blanks. Say, "Just shout out the missing part. What should it be?" (For example, "I want to _____." or "I need to _____.")

5. Have students open their books and look at the **Spotlight** box. Depending on the level and ability of the class, have students read silently, prompt different learners to read parts of the box, or read to learners.

6. Ask, "Do you have questions?" If no one has a question, ask students to do the exercises as suggested in the sections that follow.

# Spotlight Exercises

Follow these steps with the **Spotlight** exercises:

1. Whenever possible, have learners do the exercises with a partner or a small group. This allows for interaction and speaking practice. Assign partners or, if the class interacts well without prompting, allow students to choose their partners. If some learners prefer to work alone, at least have them check their answers with a partner.

2. Read the exercise directions aloud to students and point out the completed example.

3. Model the activity and ask if learners understand.

4. Check answers by asking one student from each pair to read that pair's sentences to the class.

5. Allow for differences. Some students may be especially interested in learning forms and may want you to create charts of language forms on the board, on an overhead transparency, or on handouts.

# Person to Person

Listening and speaking skills are developed further in the **Person to Person** activities, which present recorded two-person conversations exploring the unit topics in natural, colloquial language. Students listen to conversations, practice them, and work in pairs to complete a final open-ended dialogue. Students can then present their new conversations to the class.

Have students listen first, rather than read, in order to focus on the meaning of each conversation. Read or play the tape for each conversation separately. Ask learners if you should repeat the conversations or replay the tape. Ask some general questions (such as "Who are the speakers?") to check comprehension. Have learners practice words and phrases after you. You may wish to avoid having them read at this point.

Have students practice each conversation in pairs. Then ask for volunteers to role-play each conversation. Reluctant students will be more likely to participate after eager volunteers have done so.

Some students may not want to do the final, creative conversation, and it is better not to force the issue. Instead, you may wish to have learners again volunteer to perform conversations for the class.

Try to check the conversations learners create before they present them to the class so that errors are not internalized by listeners. Of course, even after you check the conversations, presentations will quite likely have some errors, but resist the temptation to correct as learners speak. A better approach is to take notes on the errors and provide these to students later, along with positive comments on their performances.

To extend the **Person to Person** activities, have learners record their conversations on an audiocassette player. Then play all the conversations for the class. Also, you may wish to have learners write their final conversation. You can then put all the papers into a box and ask each pair of learners to draw out a conversation, practice it, and perform it for the class. If appropriate, ask listeners to try to guess the authors of each conversation based on content clues.

# Reading for Real

*Contemporary English* helps students develop their reading skills and become motivated readers of English through **Reading for Real,** a page in each unit that provides stimulating authentic or adapted texts. With passages and realia that typically relate directly to the lives of characters in the **Scenes, Reading for Real** includes such real-life documents as a winning job résumé, instructions for office voice mail, biographies of real people, advice from the local police, and listings of music festivals around the country. Follow-up activities (such as **Your Turn** and **In Your Experience**) extend and personalize the reading.

Before beginning **Reading for Real,** try the following:

1. Prepare students by asking them to look at the pictures and the realia on the page.
2. Have them glance at the reading and ask questions such as the following:
   - What is this? (a bill? a résumé?)
   - Have you ever seen anything like this before?
   - Have you ever gotten one of these?
   - How does it relate to what we've been doing?
   - Why are you looking at this?
   - What will you read to find out?

Continue with the following steps:

# Books 1 and 2

1. Read the text aloud.
2. Check students' comprehension.
3. Encourage the class to talk about the topic by asking questions.
4. Record ideas on the board or a flipchart.

# Books 3 and 4

1. Ask learners to scan for specific pieces of information. With less advanced students you may wish just to call out words and have students circle them.
2. Tell students to read silently without stopping.
3. After they read, ask them to check a maximum of three words they don't know. Tell them you will talk about the words as a class later.
4. Emphasize to learners that things can—and should—be read more than once. Tell them that even the best readers don't remember everything the first time and that those readers reread difficult sections automatically.
5. Finally, stress that they don't have to worry about not being able to pronounce all the words at the beginning.
6. After **Reading for Real, Your Turn,** and **In Your Experience,** extend and personalize the reading. For example, after reading a brief résumé prepared by one character, students, with the help of a partner, use the model provided to write their own résumés. Partners then meet with another pair, exchange résumés, and make suggestions or corrections.

# Culture Corner

**Culture Corner** provides further work on reading skills by focusing on the useful inside information about U.S. life that students love. Presented as brief readings typically paired with charts, graphics, or artwork, **Culture Corner** gives students the information they need to adapt to a culture that can often be confusing and difficult to understand. Interactive follow-up activities help students integrate cultural knowledge with their language skills.

The following steps will be useful in implementing **Culture Corner:**

1. Have students look at the illustration or diagram.
2. Ask questions that encourage thoughtful guessing. If some students are advanced enough to ask others questions, encourage them to do so.
3. Have learners read the short text silently on their own.
4. When students finish, read the text aloud to them and check their comprehension.
5. Ask learners to create one or two questions about the text and ask a partner those questions.
6. If possible, have the pairs of students write their questions and answers.

As an extension activity for the **Culture Corner,** you may wish to do the following, at least in some units: Draw a simple T-chart or Venn diagram on the board or distribute copies of one of these generic organizer masters as a handout. Then ask students to compare some aspect of life in the United States to life in their native countries.

## Unit Follow-up

After learners have recorded their progress, you may wish to talk about the following in class:

- what students thought was the most important thing they learned in the unit
- what part of the unit they enjoyed most
- other situations in which they could use the same skills and strategies
- other previously mastered skills and strategies that could relate to the content of the unit just studied

In the beginning some of this may be difficult for students. Remind them to continue using previously introduced strategies and skills as they add new ones. As they progress through the book, they will expand their repertory of learning strategies.

Finally, before moving to a new unit, ask learners if they would like to do anything different the next time. Try to respect these wishes by tailoring the instruction for your learners, thus giving them a real sense of directing their own learning. The learning process will be more dynamic if these possibilities for building on experience and creating positive change can flourish in the classroom.

## Using a Problem-Posing Approach

*Contemporary English* stresses problem-solving and critical-thinking skills. Many teachers, however, may want to go beyond this framework to use a problem-posing approach, which focuses specifically on the lives of students and their own special concerns. While all of the topics in *Contemporary English* are applied to students' lives, using problem posing may help to make the connection with students' real concerns even stronger. The questions on the first page of each unit are an ideal place to begin problem posing, which involves the three following stages:

1. listening for students' concerns and issues
2. having a dialogue in which the class thinks about these issues
3. thinking about changes that people can make in their situations and suggesting a course of action

Key to this whole process is to make the discussion as learner centered as possible, so that students' issues and concerns—rather than the hypothetical or imaginary situations of characters in the text—become the focus of discussion. The text, however, can serve as a springboard for exploring students' problems since it brings into focus situations in which students and newcomers to the United States typically find themselves. Of course, students' concerns will often go beyond the context of life in the United States; and if you use problem posing, you will want to explore all of these concerns, to the extent that students find them important.

## The Audiocassettes

All key listening components of each unit are available on audiocassette. These include the **Scenes**, **Sound Bites**, **Person to Person** conversations, and the **Listen** component of the **Progress Check.**

## The Teacher's Manuals

The Teacher's Manuals give teachers additional tools to enhance learning and create an active, dynamic classroom. These include the general Introduction you are now reading for suggestions on using the approach successfully as well as unit-specific pages with teacher-friendly suggestions for preparing for, presenting, and extending activities. For ease of use, the unit-specific directions for a particular activity refer to a page of the general suggestions in this introductory unit. Many content questions that you can ask students at various points in the unit (to check comprehension and encourage application and synthesis) are also included in the unit-specific notes.

In addition, the Teacher's Manuals contain a variety of suggestions for adapting activities to the needs of multilevel classes. These suggestions are listed as Options, and they are signalled in the text by the following icon, placed in the margin:

At the end of this general introduction are two special sections: "Maximizing Results in the Multilevel Classroom" and "Creating a Work-Oriented Classroom." Written by teachers whose classroom and administrative experience makes them experts in those issues, these sections provide valuable information on using *Contemporary English* effectively in a variety of classroom settings.

## Assessment

Flexible two-page **Progress Checks** allow a program or teacher to assess learning systematically. The four sections of these tests—**Speak or Write, Listen, Language Structures,** and **Content**—can be evaluated quickly to determine readiness to move to the next unit. The **Progress Checks** are largely self-explanatory and need no special instructions here apart from a word of caution on the **Listen** section. It is best not to read the listening script slowly to accommodate learners' developing listening skills. Rather, it is better to read each passage two or three times—but always at a normal rate of speed.

## Activity Masters

Two reproducible **Activity Masters** extend each unit's learning still further. One is an interactive activity—a strip story, game, sequencing activity, or information gap—that practices language structures and reinforces content. This master can also be effective as a team-building, cooperative-learning activity. The other master— usually an additional reading or a graphic literacy activity to be completed individually or in pair or team situations— can also be used as part of the **Progress Check.**

Here are a few practical classroom management suggestions for using the **Activity Masters:**

1. Explain the general purpose of the handouts to learners. Tell them that the handouts will give them more language and vocabulary practice and allow them to share information and ideas with other learners.

2. If possible, copy the handouts on card stock so that they will be more durable and will last longer.

3. Store the masters in labeled envelopes or in a small standing or hanging file.

4. Handouts that need to be cut have dotted lines and scissors icons. Rather than cut apart your masters, whenever possible, have learners cut their individual copies. This will give them a more active role, and it will decrease your preparation time.

An additional tool for each unit is the Workbook Answers page, also on a reproducible master so that you can copy it for students if you wish them to check their own homework or one another's.

## Maximizing Results in the Multilevel Classroom

### by Elizabeth Minicz, Harper College, Palatine, Illinois

Everyone who has taught adult ESL classes is aware of the phenomenon of multilevel classes. The causes—among which are varying levels of education, disparate skill development, and open-enrollment policies—are further complicated by other factors which affect language learning, such as hemispheric dominance, personality, and sensory modality preference. Given all the challenges of a multilevel class environment, can ESL teachers rise above them to teach effectively and even enjoy the process? The answer is a resounding yes—if they have some practical tips and tools to help them perform the job.

First, recognize and accept the fact that you cannot always be all things to all students. That said, allow yourself the freedom to experiment with the techniques, methods, or "tricks of the trade" that experienced multilevel teachers discover through trial and error, and give yourself permission to fail from time to time. Some years ago, Tom Peters cautioned people in the business world to make mistakes quickly. This is sound advice for ESL teachers too; if something isn't working, try something else—immediately!

Below are some tried and true ways for you to use the realities of multilevel classes to your advantage. As you read them, you may have an occasional "Aha!" reaction—Aha, I can do that! Aha, I've done that! Aha, so that's why that works! In the end, there really is no magic answer to what to do about multilevel classes. You need to decide what works best for you, feels most comfortable, and best promotes learning. These things will always vary from teacher to teacher and class to class. Here are several approaches you should consider in using your students' variety of abilities to advantage.

## Approach I: Use a Variety of Grouping Strategies

How are grouping strategies in multilevel classes different from grouping strategies in homogeneous classes? Actually, the techniques are the same, but the purpose or intent is different. Using various grouping strategies in any class enhances learners' opportunities for practice. In multilevel classes, however, variations on grouping structures allow you to manage learner differences and abilities better. For example, separating learners according to language groups is a general grouping strategy, as are separating by gender, age, or interest. In multilevel classes, learners' abilities—which may vary according to the skill area targeted—also determine groupings. In multilevel classes, higher-level learners may be grouped together for one activity, and in another activity they may be grouped with lower-level learners.

In multilevel classes, whole-class activities can help learners develop a sense of community as they help one another succeed. They foster the "We're all in this together" feeling that temporarily overcomes individual differences. In addition, whole-class activities are confidence builders. Shy or timid learners can watch, listen, and "silently practice" until they feel comfortable participating more actively. More assertive learners can serve as role models, mentors, or tutors.

Despite these advantages of whole-class activities, if you always keep your class together, you can "miss" two-thirds of your learners because the activities are often too easy for one-third and too difficult for another third. It is important, then, to plan whole-class activities in which everyone can participate according to their individual abilities and to follow up with individual, pair, and group practice opportunities.

In *Contemporary English,* for example, the whole class looks at the pictures in a **Scene,** listens to **Sound Bites,** or reads silently. Such activities are followed by pair or group work, subsequent debriefing for the whole class, and, later, workbook activities completed at home or, if time permits, individually in class. Although in the **Scene** or **Sound Bites** all learners receive the same stimulus, individual responses will vary according to ability.

You will want to vary the pairings or groupings of learners from unit to unit, page to page, class session to class session. In homogeneous classrooms the purpose of varying groupings is simply to "mix up" the learners to avoid predictability and routine. In multilevel classes the purpose is to accommodate learner ability differences. Less able learners should have ample opportunity to work with more able learners, but not all the time!

Think through the purpose of pairings or groupings before directing your learners to work together. Arranging by categories or by assigning numbers or colors is common practice in both homogeneous and multilevel classrooms. But in homogeneous classrooms the results are random, while in multilevel classrooms you will want to determine the *who* and *why* of the groupings ahead of time. And sometimes you will want to let learners decide for themselves who they will work with.

If you are especially motivated or fond of challenges, you may have decided to use more than one level of *Contemporary English* in your class. If so, it's a good idea to begin each session with whole-class activities. Then plan to meet for 15 to 20 minutes with learners assigned to one level of the text while learners assigned to the other level(s) do pair, group, or individual work such as reading or writing. Finally, end by bringing all learners back together for a final whole-class activity. Although teaching from three levels of the series in your multilevel class is possible, two levels are undoubtedly more manageable.

## Approach 2: Adapt the Textbook Pages for Different Proficiency Levels

This approach requires more planning time than Approach 1, in which—with the exception of using two or more levels of the series in the same class—the stimuli are the same for all learners, but responses vary according to individual abilities. In Approach 1 it is your standards that must change or adjust. However, in Approach 2 the stimulus itself varies according to ability level. This means you must create or adapt tasks according to the learners' proficiencies. For example, if learners have difficulty generating language to talk about the **Scenes,** you might pose a series of yes/no, either/or, or wh-questions for them to answer first orally and then in writing.

Another way to adjust the textbook materials up or down a notch is to look closely at the tasks learners are asked to do. For example, in some **Sound Bites** activities, learners listen and write a word or phrase. You may instead want give your lower-level learners several choices and ask them to circle or check the answers—since checking or circling are easier tasks than writing words or sentences. You can also limit the number of items lower-level learners hear or, conversely, increase the number of items for higher-level learners. When in doubt, let learners decide which level of activity to complete.

Here are some additional ways to modify activities for learners' differing abilities. For the **Person to Person** activities, you can assign more advanced learners all four conversations to practice and role-play. You can ask lower-level learners to listen to all four but have them choose only one to practice and role-play. Or higher-level learners may need the additional challenge of writing more than one original conversation in **Your Turn,** whereas lower-level learners may need to have the **Your Turn** structured more tightly, with specific questions and responses that you provide.

On the **Spotlight** pages have lower-level learners work together to complete the exercises but let higher-level learners work alone. Also, you may want them to act as your aides by helping you spot-check other learners' work.

As you teach from the series, you will discover on your own more ways to add to or reduce the language load for learners.

## Approach 3: Structure Activities So That All Proficiency Levels Can Participate

Several kinds of activities can be particularly effective in multilevel classes. For example, you can provide learners with grammar practice by writing sentences and questions from **Spotlight, Reading for Real,** or **Issues and Answers** on sentence strips. Cut the strips into individual words, phrases, or clauses. Clip the words from each sentence together or put each sentence in a separate envelope. Give learners the sentences to unscramble according to their ability levels, with longer sentences going to higher-level learners and shorter ones to lower-level learners. These strips are worth the time you take to make them because they can be used over and over again. To increase the longevity of the strips, use cardboard or laminate them.

Activities involving sorting or categorizing and variations on vocabulary bingo are easy to prepare and provide meaningful practice for learners in multi-level classes. For each new unit copy **Activity Master 8-2** from the Book 1 Teacher's Manual, write the vocabulary words for the unit in the bingo squares and duplicate the page for learners' independent, pair, or group work. Then give learners scissors and have them cut out the word squares. Have them use these words for several sorts: words they know how to pronounce, words they know the meanings of, and words they can use in sentences. Otherwise, they can also use the words for alphabetizing practice. Or learners can scramble the words, put them in a pile, and take turns turning over a word, spelling it, or using it correctly in a sentence. The variations are endless.

Traditional vocabulary bingo uses an enjoyable format to provide learners with scanning practice. To play vocabulary bingo, use the same generic reproducible master mentioned above. Make the game challenging for different levels of learners by having higher-level learners pronounce, spell, and give definitions. Have lower-level learners simply say or spell the words.

In short, to maximize the effectiveness of *Contemporary English* in multilevel classes, you will need to be creative and flexible, and once you have found new ways to implement activities, share your innovations and successes with your colleagues!

# Suggestions for Creating a Work-Oriented ESL Classroom

**by Jan Jarrell, San Diego Community Colleges**

In the last decade, modeling and practicing workplace tasks and situations have become increasingly important components of the adult ESL classroom. This trend—together with the related tendency toward increased accountability—has been prompted by three interrelated societal shifts: (1) welfare reform, (2) governmental pressure on educational institutions to link funding to outcomes, and (3) the changing nature of the workplace as described in the 1992 Secretary of Labor's Commission on Achieving Necessary Skills (SCANS) Report.

## Brief Background and Description of SCANS

In the late 1980s the United States found itself playing catch-up with two booming economies: Germany's and Japan's. Comparisons of work practices in these three countries became commonplace, and as a result, many U.S. companies switched to Japanese-style management practices known as Total Quality Management (TQM). This approach coupled an emphasis on teamwork with quality control at the level of the individual employee. In response to these dramatic changes on shop floors as well as in boardrooms, the U.S. Secretary of Labor organized a national commission to identify what the new high performance workplace demanded from workers.

The fruit of this Commission was the SCANS report, which identified two tiers of essential workplace know-how: foundation skills and workplace competencies. Foundation skills include basic communication and math, as well as higher-level thinking, decision making and learning-how-to-learn skills. Personal qualities such as positive attitude, self esteem, and individual responsibility are also considered foundational. The higher-order workplace competencies include understanding and effectively using resources, technology, information, and systems. In addition, workers need effective interpersonal skills so they can work on teams, teach others, negotiate, serve customers and collaborate on the job with people from diverse backgrounds.

Continued study of workplace needs and trends since 1992 has confirmed the relevance, indeed the necessity, of integrating the SCANS competencies into the curriculum at every educational level. In order for ESL students to get and keep jobs even at the entry level, teaching the SCANS is no longer optional. Many ESL programs in states with significant second-language populations have partially or completely integrated SCANS competencies into their curricula to meet these new challenges.

## Promoting Teamwork in the Classroom

Of all the SCANS competencies, learning to work effectively in teams is perhaps the most pivotal. Teamwork either directly or indirectly drives most of the other SCANS skills, and yet many ESL students have had very little experience working in teams in their own countries—either in the classroom or on the job.

The most obvious and pedagogically familiar way of promoting teamwork in the classroom is by integrating cooperative-learning structures into your lessons. According to Johnson, Johnson, and Smith (1991), cooperative learning can be distinguished from other pair or group work because it includes five key elements:

- **Positive Interdependence:** The success of each team member and that of the team in general depends upon the effectiveness of all team members. By promoting activities such as jigsaws, which, because no student has all the information, encourage sharing of knowledge and resources, and by assigning group roles, you can allow work in teams to emerge naturally in your classroom.
- **Individual Accountability:** Structure activities so that all students must contribute. Assessing both individuals and groups assures that all learners must participate.
- **Group Processing:** Regularly provide time for team reflection and evaluation.
- **Social Skills:** Through your explicit teaching, modeling, and reinforcement, your learners can learn to lead, build trust, make decisions, and deal with conflicts.
- **Face-to-Face Interaction:** If you physically arrange learners to facilitate active involvement with one another as they discuss, teach, encourage, solve problems and negotiate, you will enhance team spirit in your classroom. In cooperative learning jigsaw activities, for example, students master content in expert groups, and then return to home groups to teach the content they have learned and also to learn new content from their teammates. As such, positive interdependence, new social skills, and face-to-face interaction are built into the activity. Later, you can assess individuals on all the content and ask the different groups to evaluate the strengths and weaknesses of their group interaction. This allows you to build in the other two elements: individual accountability and group processing.

## Team Roles

In the work-centered ESL classroom, you can assign individual team members workplace roles. For example, in a group task, each team can be comprised of a manager or leader, a secretary, a supply clerk and a timekeeper. The manager must make sure that everyone participates and may also present the group's findings to the whole class. The secretary records and reports the group's answers. The supply clerk makes sure each group member has the necessary materials and also collects and returns texts and papers at the end of the task. The timekeeper keeps the team on task by reminding members how much time remains for completing each activity. You can assign some or all of these roles on a class-by-class basis, or they can continue over a period of time. If students take roles for one or two months, you can periodically have "managers' meetings" in which assignments or problems can be discussed among the team managers who then report back to their respective teams.

Just like roles in the actual workplace, these roles are flexible, and the titles or jobs that learners assume can vary by project and possibly by geographical area or by preparation of learners for a particular sector of the economy. Having a secretary may be meaningful when many learners will be pursing an office skills track; similarly, the roles of recorder and reporter may be relevant for later involvement in community service projects. The choice of roles really depends upon you and the specifics of the business environment in your area.

## Using the Reality of the Classroom

As SCANS and the workplace become more of an influence on classroom instruction, ESL instructors are often pleased to find that daily operations of the ESL classroom provide many opportunities for students to gain actual work experience. These tasks shift responsibility for the ESL class away from you and toward students themselves. In the workplace-centered classroom, you as the instructor become a facilitator rather than a performer or directive manager.

**Classroom Management.** You can assign many classroom maintenance tasks to student teams. Team members can check signatures on the sign-in sheet, welcome new students, erase boards, and straighten chairs. They can distribute, count, and collect textbooks and set up and test equipment such as overhead projectors and audiocassette recorders. You can ensure that this work is shared and completed by posting work schedules that indicate which teams are responsible for classroom maintenance tasks on any given week or day.

**Students as Trainers.** You may wish to identify classroom procedures that students can teach new members of the class. Examples of these procedures are explaining class rules, showing newcomers how to fill out registration cards, and demonstrating for them how to turn on a computer or load a software program. Peer revision is another excellent example of how all students can function as trainers for one another.

**Solving Classroom Challenges.** It's a fact that certain challenges arise all too often in the ESL classroom. Insufficient or uncomfortable work space, inappropriate first-language use in the classroom, teams' failure to fulfill their classroom duties—all of these may seem to be inevitable features of the adult ESL classroom. But instead of first defining and then solving these problems for learners, you can turn them into resources by involving your learners actively in the problem-solving process. School or classroom issues can be identified through an anonymous suggestion box or evaluation form. Then, in teams, students can list possible solutions to the problem, discuss positive and negative consequences of each solution, and finally choose one of these solutions, implement it, and evaluate the results either as individuals or in groups. After students implement the solution, the results can be evaluated either by individuals or in groups. As an alternative, try holding class meetings in which one representative from each team participates in a brainstorming session while the rest of the class observes and later offers feedback to the meeting participants.

Of course, other problems occur on an individual or personal level, and students need to be armed with strategies to handle them. When a technological problem such as a computer failure occurs, you can encourage students to troubleshoot by following an established procedure. You can also teach teams a process for dealing with interpersonal conflict without your intervention. For example, you can train students in a round-robin exercise procedure in which each team member has two minutes to talk without interruption about what he or she thinks the problem is. Sometimes simply airing problems in this safe way will significantly diffuse negative feelings. Following the round-robin, individual team members can also write their suggestions for solving the problem that has been identified, the team secretary or reporter can read the suggestions, and all members can then discuss them.

# Emphasizing Accountability

**Using Agendas.** One easy way of keeping a class on track and modeling workplace procedures is to post an *agenda* at the start of each class. The agenda can be simply a numbered or bulleted list, or it also can indicate time frames for each activity. As each task is completed, you can check it off on the chalkboard and have students mark their ESL notebooks. At the end of class, you and your students can use the agenda to review what has been learned that day. Highlight any items that were not addressed and indicate when they will be included.

**Checklists and Logs.** Just as employees often need to account for how they spend time on the job, students can learn to monitor their own progress by marking checklists of skills, competencies, and objectives such as the **Think About Learning** chart at the end of each unit of the student books in this series. You may also wish to have students keep a daily or weekly log of what they study and accomplish.

**Evaluation.** Evaluation not only allows you to assess students' learning and interests, it also encourages critical thinking and decision making, two important SCANS skills. Evaluation can be formal or spontaneous, but it is an essential element of any work-centered classroom. It can be designed either to help the learner think about his or her own learning or to help the instructor quantify that learning.

On the formal end, instructors can prepare class evaluations in which students rate specific class activities on a scale. Students need to practice providing feedback because in the workplace they will often be asked to evaluate training they receive. Students can also grade themselves in mock performance self-appraisals. The **Think About Learning** component for each unit of this series can serve this purpose.

Less formally, you can also "check in" with students by simply distributing index cards at the end of a class period. On one side have students write what they found particularly helpful that day, and on the other side ask them to note what was unclear—or what they would like to study next. Finally, to raise students' own consciousness about the SCANS competencies, you may want to create a class poster of the SCANS using level-appropriate language or pictures. Then, at the end of each class, ask students which skills they practiced that day.

**Classroom Incentives.** Many businesses have an "Employee of the Month" award, typically for an exceptional worker, who gets his or her picture and biography posted on a special bulletin board. You can adopt this practice quite easily in the classroom by recognizing an individual student or a team each month. You may also want to present end-of-term certificates for attendance, punctuality, outstanding performance, "best suggestions," and so on. In addition, you can give letters of recommendation instead of, or in addition to, certificates. Students appreciate "to whom it may concern" letters that describe their strengths—such as being punctual or being a team player. These letters reaffirm the SCANS competencies, and students can actually use them to get jobs in the real world!

**Workplace Language.** All the suggestions outlined in this section provide students with learning experiences that can help them develop essential skills for the workplace. However, most of these strategies require systematic modeling and practice. For example, students need to be explicitly taught language to facilitate teamwork. They need to know how to agree and disagree politely, ask for repetition or clarification, and give instructions. For example, one of many employers' most frequent complaints is that employees do not let their supervisors know when they don't understand an instruction or procedure. As work-centered activities are implemented in the classroom, encourage students to use clarification strategies such as asking questions and paraphrasing instructions. By practicing the language that characterizes this new classroom environment, your learners will be actively preparing for the world of work. If you can help them to articulate these newfound skills to prospective employers, their chances of turning a job interview into a job offer can increase dramatically.

# Organization of the Unit-Specific Materials in the Teacher's Manual

In the pages that follow, the teacher's material for each unit is arranged in the following order.

1. Overview

   A. Objectives

      • Skills and Structures

      • SCANS Competencies

   B. Realia

2. Unit-specific Activity Notes (with answers for student book exercises and indicators for when to use workbook pages)

3. Answers to **Progress Checks** and **Activity Masters**

4. Workbook Answers (provided on a separate, reproducible page)

5. Unit **Progress Checks**

6. Two reproducible **Activity Masters** (Note: teacher directions—in addition to the teacher and student directions that appear on the master itself—for some of the **Activity Masters** are provided in the teacher notes at the first point in the unit where the activity can be used).

# Administering and Scoring the Placement Test

Allow 35 minutes for completion of the Placement Test. Use the Scoring Guide and the Answer Key below to score the tests.

## Scoring Guide

| Scores | Book | Level |
|---|---|---|
| 0–3 | Literacy | beginning literacy to literacy level |
| 3–7 | Book 1 | low beginning level |
| 8–17 | Book 2 | high beginning level |
| 18–25 | Book 3 | low intermediate level |
| 26–30 | Book 4 | high intermediate level |

## Answer Key

### Part 1

| | | | | |
|---|---|---|---|---|
| 1. d | 2. c | 3. b | 4. a | 5. c |
| 6. b | 7. c | 8. a | 9. a | 10. b |

### Part 2

| | |
|---|---|
| 11. much | 12. did |
| 13. are | 14. wasn't *or* was not |
| 15. Where | 16. were |
| 17. Have | 18. did |
| 19. shouldn't *or* should not | 20. am |

### Part 3

| | | | | |
|---|---|---|---|---|
| 21. d | 22. c | 23. c | 24. b | 25. c |
| 26. c | 27. b | 28. c | 29. c | 30. c |

Name _____  Date _____

# CONTEMPORARY ENGLISH PLACEMENT TEST

**Examples**

1. Complete the sentence. Circle the correct letter.

   What ___ you do in the mornings?

     a. do      b. does      c. are      d. am

2. Complete the conversation. Circle the correct letter.

   A: Are you from Algeria?

   B: Yes, I ___.

       a. is      b. are      c. am      d. be

## Part I

1. Complete the conversation. Circle the correct letter.

   A: I took a vacation last week.

   B: Oh, really? ___

     a. Where did you went?      b. Where does you go?

     c. Where go you?      d. Where did you go?

2. Complete the conversation. Circle the correct letter.

   A: It was Alice's birthday last week.

   B: Oh, really? Did she get any interesting presents?

   A: Yes, ____

     a. Tom bought to her a beautiful lamp.

     b. Tom bought a beautiful lamp to her.

     c. Tom bought her a beautiful lamp.

     d. Tom bought a beautiful lamp her.

3. Complete the conversation. Circle the correct letter.

   A: Excuse me. ___ borrow your pen?

   B: Sure, no problem. Here you are.

     a. Do I      b. Could I

     c. Would I      d. Should I

4. Complete the conversation. Circle the correct letter.

   A: Can you help me? I need ___ box up there, but I can't reach it.

   B: Sure, I'll get it down for you.

     a. that    b. this      c. these      d. those

5. Complete the conversation. Circle the correct letter.

   A: My car is getting really old.

   B: I know. You ___ get a new one.

     a. would     b. may     c. should     d. need

6. Complete the sentence.

   Have you ever ___ any repair work on your car?

     a. did     b. done     c. does     d. do

7. Complete the conversation. Circle the correct letter.

   A: There are so many dresses here, and I like all of them. I don't know which one to choose.

   B: Oh, I think this one is the ___

     a. better     . b. good     c. best     d. well.

8. Complete the conversation. Circle the correct letter.

   A: Where are you from?

   B: I'm from Spain.

   A: Oh, I have never ___ to Spain.

     a. been     b. being     c. be     d. was

9. Complete the conversation. Circle the correct letter.

   A: How is your daughter doing in school?

   B: Oh, she's doing fine. In fact, she's ___ than many of the other kids in her class.

     a. better     b. best     c. good     d. well

10. Complete the conversation. Circle the correct letter.

   A: You should stop ___ those boxes like that.

   B: Why?

   A: You'll hurt your back.

     a. to lift     b. lifting     c. lift     d. lifted

# Part 2

**Example**

   Complete the conversation. Fill in the blank.

   A: _____*What*_____ is your name?

   B: Maria.

11. Complete the conversation. Fill in the blank.

   A: How _____ coffee do you want?

   B: About a pound.

12. Complete the conversation. Fill in the blank.

   A: Where _____ you live in your native country?

   B: I lived in Mexico City.

13. Complete the conversation. Fill in the blank.

 A: What _____ you going to do tomorrow?

 B: I'm going to a movie.

14. Complete the conversation. Fill in the blank.

 A: Were you here yesterday?

 B: No, I _____.

15. Complete the conversation. Fill in the blank.

 A: _____ do you live?

 B: I live in Miami.

16. Complete the sentence. Fill in the blank.

 What _____ you doing when you saw the accident?

17. Complete the conversation. Fill in the blank.

 A: _____ you ever worked in a bank before?

 B: No, I used to work as a cashier, but that was in a restaurant.

18. Complete the conversation. Fill in the blank.

 A: When _____ you talk to the boss about this matter?

 B: Only yesterday.

19. Complete the conversation. Fill in the blank.

 A: This letter says I've won a million dollars, but I have to buy some magazines to get the money. Do you think I should do that?

 B: No, you _____.

20. Complete the sentence. Fill in the blank.

 I _____ never going to understand this tax form. It's too complicated.

# Part 3

**To answer questions 21 and 22, read the following ad.**

S A L E ! ! !  S A L E ! ! !  S A L E ! ! !
Peaches 10 cents each
Tomatoes 29 cents a pound
Red apples 5 cents each

21. You want to buy four peaches. How much will you pay? Circle the correct letter.

 a. 10 cents    b. 20 cents    c. 30 cents    d. 40 cents

22. You want to buy two pounds of tomatoes. How much will you pay? Circle the correct letter.

 a. 39 cents    b. 60 cents    c. 58 cents    d. 5 cents

To answer questions 23–25, read the memo and the story after it.

> # MEMO
>
> **TO:** All employees
>
> **FROM:** Mark
>
> **RE:** Vacation time
>
> Beginning in January of next year, Bestco Inc. will shift to the following vacation schedule.
>
> Employees with up to 1 year of service:
> 1 week per year
>
> Employees with 2–4 years of service:
> 2 weeks per year
>
> Employees with 5 to 10 years of service:
> 3 weeks per year
>
> Employees with more than 10 years of service:
> 4 weeks per year

Frank Malyszko started at Bestco at the beginning of this year. His friend Juan started two years ago. Right now, Frank has three vacation days, and Juan has a week.

23. How much vacation time will Frank have next year? Circle the correct letter.

    a. He will have one week.

    b. He will have two weeks.

    c. He will have three weeks.

    d. He will have four weeks.

24. How much vacation time will Juan have next year? Circle the correct letter.

    a. He will have one week.

    b. He will have two weeks.

    c. He will have three weeks.

    d. He will have four weeks.

25. How much vacation time does an employee get after 8 years? Circle the correct letter.

    a. one week

    b. two weeks

    c. three weeks

    d. four weeks

**To answer questions 26 and 27, read the following memo.**

---

# MEMO

**TO:**      All employees

**FROM:**   James Ross

**RE**        Changes in Health Plan

Please note the following:

Those employees who now have REGNA Health Care will have to switch to a new company. Employees will be able to choose between HealthPrev Company, Keystone Health Maintenance, and Arbco Health. Here are the costs for each of these plans:

| | | |
|---|---|---|
| **HealthPrev Company** | Family Plan: | $205.00/month for a family with children |
| | Joint Plan: | $140.00/month for a couple without children |
| | Single Plan: | $105.00/month for a single employee |
| **Keystone Health** | Family Plan: | $180.00/month for a family with children |
| | Joint Plan: | $150.00/month for a couple without children |
| | Single Plan: | $90.00/month for a single employee |
| **Arbco Health** | Family Plan: | $200.00/month for a family with children |
| | Joint Plan: | $160.00/month for a couple without children |
| | Single Plan: | $80.00/month for a single employee |

Employees who currently have the REGNA plan may wish to discuss it with other employees who already have one of the other three plans above.

---

26. Which of the plans is the cheapest for a single employee? Circle the correct letter.

    a. Keystone Health

    b. HealthPrev Company

    c. Arbco Health

    d. They are all the same.

27. Which of the plans is the most expensive for a family with children? Circle the correct letter.

    a. Keystone Health

    b. HealthPrev Company

    c. Arbco Health

    d. They are all the same.

**To answer questions 28–30, read the following passage.**

What do you need to do to stay healthy? Well, diet and exercise play an important role, but an important factor is avoiding things that can hurt your health. For example, if you smoke cigarettes, you have a much greater risk of heart disease and cancer than nonsmokers. Alcohol can also increase your risk for these health problems if you have several drinks each day, for example, and it can lead to liver problems also. Doctors are unsure about the risk of having only one drink a day. Drinking coffee presents some of the same risks as smoking, but smoking is worse for you. Doctors caution us to keep our consumption of caffeine low, but many Americans drink three or four cups of coffee a day, or more.

28. Which of the following health problems is not mentioned in the passage above?

    a. heart disease

    b. cancer

    c. diabetes

    d. liver problems

29. What are the health risks of having one drink a day?

    a. very serious

    b. heart disease

    c. unclear

    d. no risk at all

30. If "many Americans drink three or four cups of coffee a day, or more," which of the following is probably true?

    a. This is more of a problem than smoking cigarettes.

    b. This is not a problem for people who don't smoke.

    c. This is more than doctors think they should drink.

    d. There are no serious health risks in drinking coffee.

# Unit A

# OVERVIEW

## Objectives

### Skills and Structures

Use eye movement from left to right, top to bottom

Discriminate between uppercase letters

Trace uppercase letters following guide arrows

Copy uppercase letters of the alphabet

Relate phonological sounds to letters

Recognize words on common signs

Trace words on common signs

Respond to simple commands

### SCANS Competencies

Foundation Skills

### Realia

Magazines, newspapers, and ads (from which students can cut letters)

# ACTIVITY NOTES

### Page 1

## Exercise 1

**Refer to the general instructions on page xii in the Introduction.**

### Preparation

1. Before having students begin to work in the textbook, introduce each of the letters on the page-*L, T, I, H*. Write the first letter on the board: *L*. Say the name of the letter and model the sound. Choose or invite students to choose a common word that begins with *L* such as *listen, look, left,* or *leg*. The word should be relevant to the students' lives or easily acted out.

2. Model tracing the letter on the board (be sure to use the uppercase form of the letter) and have students follow the same movements in the air. Use direction words (*down, across,* etc.) as you trace the letter to show the direction of the strokes. Then say the letter name, sound, and word. Ask students to repeat. Repeat this step several times as needed.

3. Encourage students to give the letter name, sound, and word as you point to the example of the letter on the board. Use gestures and word cues as needed: ("What's its name?" ("L.") Cup your hand behind your ear. "(What's the) sound?" /l/ Point to object or mime action. "(What's the) word?" "Look."

4. Introduce the other letters on the page, using the same procedure: *T, I, H*. Some useful words might be: *T—telephone, teacher, table; I—in, inch, clip; H—hat, hot, happy, hospital*. For this level, introduce only the short vowel sound for the letter *I*.

5. Point to one of the letters on the board and then point out one or two examples of the letter on signs or papers around the room. Invite students to find other examples of the letter. Repeat with the other letters.

### Presentation

1. Write the first line of the exercise on the board. Model the exercise. Demonstrate going from left to right as you do the exercise on the board. Note that it is not necessary for students to read the words. The focus is just to have them look for and circle the appropriate letters in the words.

2. Have students work individually or in pairs to complete the exercise. Go around the room, helping students as needed. If students have difficulty with left-to-right directionality, have them use a ruler or strip of paper to guide them with the lines of the exercise.

3. Write the rest of the exercise on the board and ask volunteers to come to the board and circle the correct letters. Students can check their own work.

### Extension

 **Option:** In mixed-literacy level classes, you may want to have students work on the alphabet and numbers in Book 1, Introductory Unit pages viii and ix, simultaneously with this unit.

### Answers to Exercise 1

| | | | |
|---|---|---|---|
| ⓁEFT | POⓁICE | WAⓁK | |
| ⓉOP | LEⓉⓉER | DAⓉE | |
| ⒾCE | APRⒾL | ⒾN | CLⒾNⒾC |
| ⒽOT | RIGⒽT | ⒽOSPITAL | |

# Exercise 2

**Refer to the general instructions on page xii in the Introduction.**

### Presentation

1. Write the first line of the exercise on the board. Model writing the letter across the line. Remind students of the directions for the strokes of each letter.

2. Students can complete the exercise individually. Encourage students to say letter names, sounds, and words as they write the letters.

3. Go around the room. Observe how students hold pencils and pens. Help students as needed. If students have difficulty, you may want to have them practice writing horizontal and vertical lines in a variety of ways: writing them on the board or in the air, tracing letters with a finger, etc.

### Answers to Exercise 2

L, I, T, H

Page 2

# Exercise 3

**Refer to the general instructions on page xii in the Introduction.**

### Preparation

1. Review the letters *L, T, I, H.* Invite students to come to the board and write the letters. Ask students to give letter names, sounds, and words.

2. Introduce the letters: *E, F, K, X*. These letters use horizontal, vertical, and some diagonal lines. Repeat the procedure used to introduce the first set of letters. Some useful words might be the following: *E—egg, exit, elephant, enter; F—fire, fat, fish; K—key, kid, kitchen; X—x-ray, exit.* (NOTE: Introduce the short vowel sound of *e*. The long vowel sounds can be pointed out at a later time.)

## Presentation

1. Have students work individually or in pairs to complete the exercise. Go around the room, helping students as needed.

2. Write the exercise on the board and ask volunteers to come to the board and circle the correct letters. Students can check their own work. Review letter names, sounds, and words again.

### Answers to Exercise 3

EMPLOYEE    ENTER    EXIT
FIRE        OFF      OFFICE
KID         BANK     NICKEL
X-RAY       EXIT     TAXI

# Exercise 4

**Refer to the general instructions on page xii in the Introduction.**

## Preparation

Model writing the letters on the board again before having students complete the exercise individually. Encourage students to say letter names, sounds, and words as they write the letters.

## Presentation

Go around the room helping students as needed.

## Extension

Have students write the letters they have learned on index cards. On the opposite side, students can illustrate the words for the letters. Students can work in pairs to practice letter names, sounds, and words.

### Answers to Exercise 4

E, F, K, X

# Exercise 5

**Refer to the general instructions on page xii in the Introduction.**

## Preparation

1. Review previously taught letters: letter names, sounds, and words. Use a variety of activities. For example: Say a letter name and have students point to an example or hold up a letter card. Write a letter on the board and have students supply the letter name, sound, and word. Say a letter and have a student write it on the board.

2. Introduce the letters: *A, M, V, N*. Repeat the procedure that was used to introduce the other sets of letters. Some useful words might be the following: *A—apple, address; M—man, money, map; V—van, vegetable, Vietnam; N—no, name, nose.*

### Presentation

1. Have students work individually or in pairs to complete the exercise. Go around the room, helping students as needed.

2. Write the exercise on the board and ask volunteers to come to the board and circle the correct letters. Students can check their own work. Review letter names, sounds, and words again.

### Answers to Exercise 5

ⒶGE     NⒶME     ⒶPⒶRTMENT
Ⓜ EN     LIⓂ IT     WOⓂ EN
Ⓥ ERY     LIⓋ E     NOⓋ EMBER
Ⓝ O     DOⓃ 'T     OⓃ        ⓃUMBER

# Exercise 6

**Refer to the general instructions on page xii in the Introduction.**

### Presentation

1. Model writing the letters on the board. Then have students complete the exercise individually. Encourage students to practice the letter names, sounds, and words as they trace and write the letters.

2. Go around the room helping as needed.

### Extension

Invite students to look through newspapers, ads, or magazines for examples of the various letters. Students can cut out the letters. Help students create collages for each of the letters. Have students notice the variety of print: size, font styles, and colors.

### Answers to Exercise 6

A, M, V, N

# Exercise 7

**Refer to the general instructions on page xii in the Introduction.**

### Preparation

1. Review previously taught letters: letter names, sounds, and words. Invite volunteers to take on the role of teacher to quiz others in the review.

2. Introduce the letters: *C, O, U, G.* These letters use curved lines. If needed, spend some time having students drawing curved lines in the air, on the board, or on paper before proceeding to the letters. Repeat the procedure that was used to introduce the other sets of letters. Some useful words might be the following: *C—cold, car, cat, coffee; O—on, off; U—up, umbrella, under; G—go, good, gas.* (NOTE: Focus on just the hard sounds of the letters C and G. The soft sounds can be pointed out later as exceptions.)

### Presentation

1. Have students work individually or in pairs to complete the exercise. Go around the room, helping students as needed.

2. Write the exercise on the board and ask volunteers to come to the board to circle the correct letters. Students can check their own work.

**Answers to Exercise 7**

ⒸLINIⒸ    SⒸHOOL    ⒸLOSED
ⓄUT        ⓄCTⓄBER   DⓄCTⓄR
ⓊP         TUⓇN       SⓊNDAY    Ⓤ.S.A.
ⒼO         AⒼE        ⒼAS        EⒼⒼS

# Exercise 8

Refer to the general instructions on page xii in the Introduction.

## Presentation

1. Model writing the letters on the board. Then have students complete the exercise individually. Encourage students to practice the letter names, sounds, and words as they trace and write the letters.

2. Go around the room helping as needed.

## Extension

Have the class take a walk around the building or neighborhood. Invite students to point out and identify various letters that they see.

## Answers to Exercise 8

C, O, U, G

Page 5

# Exercise 9

Refer to the general instructions on page xii in the Introduction.

## Preparation

1. Review previously taught letters: letter names, sounds, and words. Provide a variety of review activities.

2. Introduce the letters: *S, D, P, B, R*. Most of these letters combine curved and straight lines. Repeat the procedure that was used to introduce the other sets of letters. Some useful words might be the following: *S—sit, stop, sad; D—down, doctor; P—pen, pencil, paper, post office; B—bag, baby, bus; R—read, red, right.*

3. Have students work individually or in pairs to complete the exercise. Go around the room, helping students as needed.

4. Write the exercise on the board and ask volunteers to come to the board and circle the correct letters. Students can check their own work.

## Answers to Exercise 9

ⓈTOP      PAⓈⓈING    ⓈTATE
ⒹON'T     AⒹⒹRESS    ⒹOCTOR
ⓅARK      UⓅ         OⓅEN
ⒷUS       JOⒷ        ⒷIRTH
ⓇEAD      LIBⓇAⓇY    ⓇIGHT

# Exercise 10

Refer to the general instructions on page xii in the Introduction.

## Presentation

1. Model writing the letters on the board. Then have students complete the exercise individually. Encourage students to practice the letter names, sounds, and words as they trace and write the letters.

2. Go around the room helping as needed.

## Extension

Write all the letters that have been studied in random order on the board. Say a letter name and have a volunteer come to the board to circle the letter. Repeat until all of the letters have been circled. (NOTE: This activity can be repeated with you saying the sounds. Students can point out or circle the correct letters.)

## Answers to Exercise 10

S, D, P, B, R

## Page 6

# Exercise 11

Refer to the general instructions on page xii in the Introduction.

## Preparation

1. Review previously taught letters: letter names, sounds, words.

2. Introduce the letters: *Q, J, W, Y, Z.* Repeat the procedure that was used to introduce the other sets of letters. Some useful words might be the following: *Q—quiet, question; J—job, jacket, juice; W—walk, woman, work, water; Y—yes, yellow, year; Z—zero, zoo, ZIP code.*

## Presentation

1. Have students work individually or in pairs to complete the exercise. Go around the room, helping students as needed.

2. Write the exercise on the board and ask volunteers to come to the board to circle the correct letters. Students can check their own work. Review letter names, sounds, and words again.

## Answers to Exercise 11

| | | |
|---|---|---|
| ⓆUIET | EⓆUAL | ⓆUARTER |
| ⒿUNE | ⒿOB | ⒿUICE |
| ⓌALK | SAⓌ | ⓌEEK |
| ⓎEAR | DAⓎ | ⓎES |
| ⓏIP CODE | SIⓏE | ⓏONE |

# Exercise 12

**Refer to the general instructions on page xii in the Introduction.**

## Presentation

Model writing the letters on the board. Then have students complete the exercise individually. Encourage students to practice letter names, sounds, and words as they trace and write the letters.

## Extension

1. Students can practice copying their own names using the uppercase letters. If needed, make dotted letters for students to trace their names.
2. Make name cards for students. Place the cards around the room. Have students find their names. Encourage students to practice saying the letters in their names.
3. Dictate the letters of a student's name. Have students arrange letter cards or write the letters. Then have the class match the name to the student in the class.

## Answers to Exercise 12

Q, J, W, Y, Z

Page 7

# Exercise 13

**Refer to the general instructions on page xii in the Introduction.**

## Preparation

1. Introduce common signs around the neighborhood. You may want to take the class on a walking tour to point out various signs. Encourage students to name letters on the signs and comment on color, location, and shape of the signs. Ask students what the signs mean. (NOTE: Students can discuss the signs in their native languages. If not, encourage students to act out or mime what the signs mean.) In this lesson, the words on common signs are going to be presented to students as sight words.
2. Write the word *UP* on a word card. Say, "Up." Have students repeat the word. Draw an arrow or point in the direction to show the meaning. Guide students to notice details of the word. Point out the first letter and have students review the letter sound. Have students notice the number of letters in the word.
3. Introduce the other sight words, using the same procedure. Use appropriate symbols or actions to clarify meanings.
4. Display the sight words on the board or around the room. Say one of the words and have students point to or go to the appropriate sight word.

## Presentation

1. Have students look at the signs and words on page 7. Tell students to trace the letters that make the words.
2. Students can use letter cards to reproduce the words on the signs.

## Extension

1. Have students make their own signs and place them in appropriate places around the room or in the building. More advanced students can copy other signs that they see outside of class and bring them in for discussion and study.

2. Depending on students' skills, students can begin a picture or word dictionary. Encourage students to write each letter on a separate piece of paper. Students may want to draw pictures or find pictures from magazines and ads to illustrate words they know that begin with each of the letters. More skilled students can copy words that they know that begin with each of the letters. Students can share their dictionaries with others in the class.

3. Students can make letter cards and use them in various practice exercises. Here are some examples:

   - Students can work in pairs or small groups to review or quiz each other on letter names, sounds, and words.

   - In groups, have students play concentration with two sets of letter cards. Mix the cards and place them in rows face down. Students take turns choosing two cards and identifying the letters. If the cards match, the student keeps the cards and goes again. If the cards don't match, the student turns the cards face down on the table again, and the next person goes. Continue until all the cards are matched.

   - Dictate letters and have students find and arrange the letter cards in proper order to match what you dictated.

## Answers to Exercise 13

up, down, stop, exit, men, women, walk, don't walk

### Page 8

# Exercise 14

**Refer to the general instructions on page xii in the Introduction.**

## Preparation

1. Introduce the new sight words, using the same procedure as for Exercise 13. Use appropriate symbols or actions to clarify meanings.
2. Display the sight words on the board or around the room. Say one of the words and have students point to or go to the appropriate sight word.
3. Point to the sight words and ask students to read them aloud and act out the sign.

## Presentation

1. Have students look at the signs and words on page 8. Tell students to trace the letters that make the words.
2. Students can use letter cards to reproduce the words on the signs.

## Extension

Have students use the letter cards they made for Exercise 13 to quiz each other on the sounds and words on page 8.

## Answers to Exercise 14

on, off, pull, push, phone, closed, hospital, school

# UNIT B

# OVERVIEW

## Objectives

### Skills and Structures

Discriminate between uppercase and lowercase letters

Match uppercase letters with corresponding lowercase letters, and vice versa

Copy uppercase and lowercase letters

Recognize alphabetical order

Count from 1–10

Discriminate among numerals

Trace and copy numerals

Follow simple directions with numbers

### SCANS Competencies

Foundation Skills

### Realia

Magazines, newspapers, and ads (from which students can cut letters)

# ACTIVITY NOTES

### Pages 9–10

## Exercise 1

**Refer to the general instructions on page xii in the Introduction.**

### Preparation

1. Review uppercase letters. Show students letter cards and have them give the letter names, sounds, and associated words.

2. Say a letter name and have students find the correct letter card. Give a letter sound and ask students to find or point to the correct letter card.

3. Introduce the lowercase letters for the letters *A–L*. Write both the upper and lowercase letters on the board. Encourage students to comment on similarities or differences between the uppercase and lowercase letters. Explain that the uppercase and lowercase letters stand for the same letter.

4. Model tracing the letters on the board (use direction words: *down, across,* etc.) and have students follow the same movements in the air or at the board.

### Presentation

1. Tell students to look at the letters on page 9. Ask students to write both the upper- and lowercase letters. Encourage them to say letter names and sounds as they work. You may want to have students work in pairs as they complete the exercise.

2. Repeat the procedure for the letters *M-Z* on page 10.

## Extension

1. Play a game with the textbook pages. Say a letter from *A–L* or *M–Z* (depending on which page is used). Students should cover the letter with a marker when they hear it. Repeat the procedure until all of the letters are covered.

2. If students have their own sets of letter cards, have them use sixteen letters to make four rows with four letters in each row. Then play letter bingo. Have one person call out letters in random order. The first person who has four in a row wins and becomes the next caller.

**Option:** In mixed-literacy level classes, you may want to have students work on the alphabet and numbers in Book 1, Introductory Unit pages viii and ix, simultaneously with this unit.

### Answers to Exercise 1

Aa, Bb, Cc, Dd, Ee, Ff, Gg, Hh, Ii, Jj, Kk, Ll, Mm, Nn, Oo, Pp, Qq, Rr, Ss, Tt, Uu, Vv, Ww, Xx, Yy, Zz

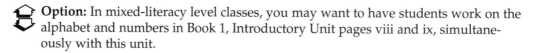

## Exercise 2

Refer to the general instructions on page xii in the Introduction.

### Preparation

1. Review uppercase and lowercase letters. Arrange uppercase letter cards on the board. Show students a lowercase letter card and have a volunteer point to the correct uppercase letter. Practice the other letters in a similar manner. Reinforce letter names, sounds, and words throughout the exercise.

### Presentation

1. Write the first line of the exercise on the board. Demonstrate the exercise. Ask a student to name the letter and point out the appropriate lowercase letter. Ask the student to circle the correct lowercase letter. Reinforce left to right directionality as you guide students through the example.

2. Have students work individually or in pairs to complete the exercise. Go around the room, helping students as needed.

3. Write the complete exercise on the board and ask volunteers to come to the board and circle the correct letters. Students can correct their own work. Review again letter names, sounds, and words.

### Answers to Exercise 2

| | | |
|---|---|---|
| a | h | (n) |
| (p) | g | r |
| t | b | (f) |
| k | (l) | i |
| u | (a) | c |
| (h) | m | d |
| e | (r) | k |

# Exercise 3

**Refer to the general instructions on page xii in the Introduction.**

## Preparation

Review lowercase letters. Hold up a lowercase letter card. Encourage students to give the name of the letter, the sound, and a word with the letter. Invite a volunteer to come to the board and write both the uppercase and lowercase letter. Continue with other letters.

## Presentation

1. Write the top half of the matching exercise on the board. Ask volunteers to name the letters in the two columns. Then demonstrate doing the exercise by drawing a line from the first uppercase letter on the left to the corresponding lowercase letter in the right column.

2. Have students work individually or in pairs to complete the two exercises. Go around the room, helping students as needed.

3. Write the exercises on the board and ask volunteers to come to the board and match the upper and lowercase letters. Students can correct their own work. Review again letter names, sounds, and words.

## Extension

1. Invite students to look through newspapers, ads, or magazines for examples of the various lowercase letters. Students can cut out the letters and add them to their letter collages or personal dictionaries.

2. Explain that the letters on pages 9 and 10 are in alphabetical order. This is the order in which the letters are usually written. Say the letters in alphabetical order, and have volunteers write the uppercase and lowercase forms on the board. Then have students work in pairs and put sets of letter cards in alphabetical order.

## Answers to Exercise 3

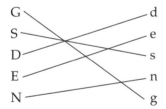

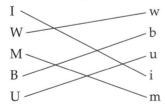

## Exercise 4
**Refer to the general instructions on page xii in the Introduction.**

### Preparation
1. Introduce counting from 1–5. Model counting using your fingers or objects in the class and then ask students to repeat. Repeat and practice as needed.
2. Write the numerals 1–5 on the board. Point to each and say the number. Ask students to repeat.
3. Say a number and have a volunteer come to the board and point to the correct numeral. Continue as needed.
4. Model writing the numerals. Give direction words as you write the numerals. Students can write the numerals in the air.

### Presentation
1. Ask students to look at page 13. Review counting 1–5. Introduce 0.
2. Tell students to trace and copy the numerals in their books. Encourage students to say the numbers as they write.

### Extension
Have students look through ads, magazines, or newspapers for numbers. Invite students to comment on variations in print: size, style, color, etc.

### Answers to Exercise 4
0, 1, 2, 3, 4, 5

## Exercise 5
**Refer to the general instructions on page xii in the Introduction.**

### Preparation
1. Review numbers 0–5. Have students count various objects in the class.
2. Write the numerals on the board. Say a number and have a volunteer point to the correct numeral. Continue as needed.
3. Introduce and practice counting from 6–10 using the same procedure from the previous page. Also introduce and practice the numbers 6–10.

### Presentation
1. Ask students to look at page 14. Review counting 6–10.
2. Tell students to write the numerals in their books. Encourage students to say the numbers as they write. Go around the room giving assistance as needed.

### Extension
1. Introduce simple directions with numbers. Give directions and have students find the correct pages in their books. For example, say "Turn to page 3. Turn to page 8."
2. Give students collections of small objects such as paper clips, pencils, coins, etc. Say numbers and have students arrange the correct number of objects.

3. Ask students to find numbers around the room such as ones on clocks, in books, on doors, on calendars. Encourage students to read the numbers aloud.

## Answers to Exercise 6

6, 7, 8, 9, 10

**Page 15**

# Exercise 6

**Refer to the general instructions on page xii in the Introduction.**

## Preparation

1. Review counting and reading numerals from 1–10.
2. Place groups of objects on a table or desk. Ask students to count the objects. Invite volunteers to write the numerals on the board.
3. Point to a numeral on the board and have students arrange the correct number of objects.

## Presentation

1. Write the first line of the exercise from page 15 on the board. Model the exercise by asking students to identify the numeral and then count out the correct number of objects. Demonstrate circling the objects.
2. Have students work individually to complete the exercise. Go around the room, helping students as needed.
3. Students can check their own work in pairs.

## Answers to Exercise 6

First Row: 8 chairs should be circled.

Second Row: 5 tables should be circled.

Third Row: 2 books should be circled.

Fourth Row: 4 cups should be circled.

Fifth Row: 10 cars should be circled.

# Exercise 7

**Refer to the general instructions on page xii in the Introduction.**

## Presentation

1. Model the matching exercise. Ask a volunteer to count the objects in the first line. Tell students to draw a line to the correct numeral.
2. Have students complete the exercise individually. Encourage students to count aloud. Go around the room helping as needed.
3. Students can check their own work in pairs.

**Answers to Exercise 7**

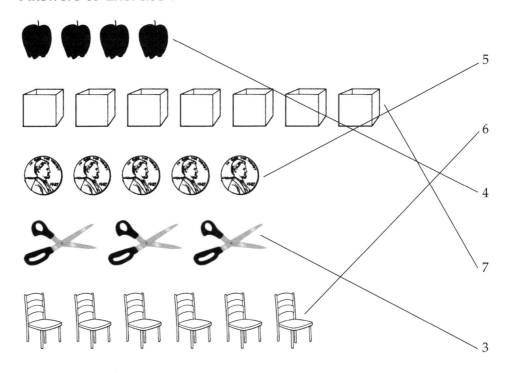

# Exercise 8

**Refer to the general instructions on page xii in the Introduction.**

## Preparation

Dictate numbers and have students write the numerals. For example: *Three* (3). *Ten* (10). For more advanced students, add an additional step by having students count out the correct number of given objects before writing the numerals.

## Presentation

1. Write the first line of the exercise on the board. Model the exercise by counting the objects in the first line and then writing the numeral at the end of the line.

2. Tell students to complete the exercise individually or in pairs. Go around the room as students work, giving assistance as needed.

3. Go over the exercise with the group. Have students check their own work.

## Answers to Exercise 8

5, 6, 2, 8, 9, 5

# Exercise 9

**Refer to the general instructions on page xii in the Introduction.**

## Presentation

1. Write the first two lines of the exercise on the board. Model the exercise by counting aloud and pointing to the numerals. Encourage students to say the missing numbers in the second line. Demonstrate writing the numerals on the blank spaces.

2. Have students complete the exercise individually. Students can check their work with a partner.

## Extension

1. Have students make number flashcards. Say numbers and ask students to hold up the correct number card. Students can practice in pairs.

2. Say groups of numbers and have students find and arrange the number cards in the correct order. For example: *One-three-five.* (1-3-5). After students can do this activity well, have students write the groups of numbers as you dictate them. (NOTE: This activity can lead into reading and writing telephone numbers.)

3. Bring in dice or playing cards (use just the number cards). Have students work in pairs rolling the dice and counting the spots. Students can practice reading numbers using the playing cards.

4. Have the class play number bingo. Students can choose nine cards to create a bingo board (three rows with three cards in each row). Call out numbers in random order. The first person to get three in a row wins and becomes the next caller.

5. Students can practice writing their names using uppercase and lowercase letters. Point out that the first letter in names should be uppercase.

6. Have students write words that they see in their everyday environment and bring them to class. Help students with meaning, and then have students share them with class, writing them on the board.

7. For students who need extra practice, present matching and completion exercises similar to those in the Student Book.

## Answers to Exercise 9

1, 4, 7, 9

2, 5, 6, 8, 9

1, 2, 3, 4, 5, 6, 7, 8, 9, 10

# UNIT 1

# WHAT'S YOUR NAME?

## OVERVIEW

## Objectives

### Skills and Structures

Identify oneself by name

Give personal information about one's first and last name

Spell one's name

Greet others

Respond to greetings

Ask and respond to questions about one's name and its spelling

Copy/write first and last name on a form

Recognize sight words: *name, first, last*

Discriminate between first and last names

Write letters from dictation

Recognize word and symbol signs for restrooms

### SCANS Competencies

Foundation Skills

### Realia

Forms and applications (on which students can write their names)

# ACTIVITY NOTES

## Spotlight

**Refer to the general instructions on page xi in the Introduction.**

### Preparation

1. Make or have students make name tags.

2. Model introducing yourself. Point to your name tag as you say, "I'm (your name)." Invite students to introduce themselves following the model.

3. Model questions and answers about name. "What's your name? I'm (My name is) ___." Ask the question and have volunteers respond with their names.

### Presentation

1. Tell students to look at the picture on page 17. Point out the people in the picture and model their names. Have students find the name tags. Encourage students to use the initial letters in the names to help remember the names.

2. Say the names of the characters and have students point to the correct person in the illustration.

3. Invite students to talk about where the people are and what they are doing. Discussion can be in students' native languages or in English depending on students' level.

## Sound Bites

**Refer to the general instructions on page ix in the Introduction.**

## Exercise I

### Presentation

1. Ask students to listen as you play the tape or read the listening script for Exercise 1.

2. Replay the tape line by line. Tell students to point to the characters who are speaking the individual lines.

## Listening Script

A: Hi! I'm Marc. What's your name?

B: My name is Sonia.

A: Nice to meet you.

B: And you.


A: Hi! My name is Anna.

B: I'm Bill.

A: This is my friend. Her name is Kim.

B: Nice to meet you.

## Page 18

# Your Turn

**Refer to the general instructions on page x in the Introduction.**

## Preparation

1. Review questions and answers about names. Say, "I'm ___. What's your name? My name is ___."
2. Ask the question and have students answer with their names. Next, invite volunteers to do the questioning.

## Presentation

1. Model the conversation. You may want to use puppets or pictures of people to present the conversation orally.
2. Play the tape or read the listening script. Have students repeat each line.
3. Students should orally practice the conversation in the book before reading the conversation using their own name.

 **Option 1:** Take the role of Marc and have the class take Sonia's role. Practice the dialogue orally.

**Option 2:** Take the role of Marc and have volunteers take the role of Sonia. Students can substitute their own names in the conversation. Then switch roles so students learn both parts of the conversation.

**Option 3:** In pairs have more advanced students practice the conversation in the book and the conversation with their own names. Have them practice several times with different partners or present their conversation to the class.

## Listening Script

A: Hi! I'm Marc. What's your name?

B: My name is Sonia.

A: Nice to meet you.

B: And you.

# Reading for Real

**Refer to the general instructions on page xii in the Introduction.**

## Preparation

1. Introduce the words *first* and *last name.* You may want to use some students' names to illustrate. Encourage students to check their Social Security cards, alien registration cards, etc., for the order of their names. (NOTE: In some cultures, the last or family name precedes the given or first name.) Practice questions and answers about first and last name.

2. Write on the board or on cards the sight words: *first, last, name.* Point out the initial consonants and help students read the words. Say the words and have students point to the correct sight words. Then point to the words and ask students to respond with the appropriate information.

## Presentation

1. Read aloud the dialogue and form as students follow along in their books. Read again and have students read along with you.

2. Ask students to point to various words in the reading selection as you say them. Then ask comprehension questions such as the following: "Point to Kim. What's her first name? What's her last name?" NOTE: Point out to students that the first letter in both the first and last names is uppercase.

## Exercise 2

**Refer to the general instructions on page xii in the Introduction.**

## Preparation

Use word cards to review the sight words: *name, first, last.* Say the words and have students point to the correct word cards.

## Presentation

1. Write the first line from the exercise on the board. Model the exercise. Ask a volunteer to read the first word in the line. Then point to each of the three other words in the line. As you point to each word, ask: "Is it the same (or different)?" If needed, point out the individual letters and the order of the letters in the words. Demonstrate circling the word that is the same as the first.

2. Have students complete the exercise. You may want to have volunteers read aloud the first word in each line before students work on their own. As students work, go around the room, helping as needed.

## Answers to Exercise 2

The following words should be circled:

1. NAME     2. FIRST     3. LAST

4. Name     5. First     6. Last

# Exercise 3

**Refer to the general instructions on page xii in the Introduction.**

## Preparation

1. Write a volunteer's full name, first name, and last name on the board.

2. Hold up the word cards: *First Name.* Ask the class which form of the student's name is the correct response. Repeat with word cards: *Last Name* and *Name.*

## Presentation

1. Have students look at the exercise. Ask questions to elicit the correct responses to the sight words. If needed, model the matching exercise on the board.

2. Students can work in pairs or individually to complete the exercise.

3. Go over the answers with the group.

## Answers to Exercise 3

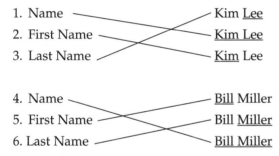

1. Name — Kim <u>Lee</u>
2. First Name — Kim Lee
3. Last Name — Kim Lee

4. Name — <u>Bill</u> Miller
5. First Name — Bill <u>Miller</u>
6. Last Name — Bill Miller

---

**Page 20**

# Sound Bites

**Refer to the general instructions on page ix in the Introduction.**

# Exercise 4

## Preparation

1. Review the letter names. Use letter cards or write the alphabet on the board. Say a letter and have volunteers come and point to the correct letter. Point out the order of the letters in alphabet. Explain that this is the common way to list the letters.

2. Practice spelling names. Have students arrange letter cards to spell out their names. Then have them practice saying the letters.

## Presentation

1. Model the exercise. Write the first item of the exercise on the board. Tell students to listen carefully for the missing letter in the name. Play the tape or read the text for the first item. Ask students which letter is missing. Invite a volunteer to come to the board and circle the letter and then write the letter in the blank space. NOTE: Point out to students that the first letter in both the first and last names is uppercase.

2. Play the rest of the exercise and have students complete the exercise in their books. Replay the cassette as needed.

3. Go over the answers with the group.

### Answers to Exercise 4

1. B, Bill        2. M, Marc        3. L, Lee
4. D, Davis       5. K, Kim         6. A, Anna

### Listening Script

1. A: My name is Bill.
   B: How do you spell it?
   A: B-I-L-L.

2. A: I'm Marc.
   B: How do you spell it?
   A: M-A-R-C.

3. A: My last name is Lee.
   B: How do you spell it?
   A: L-E-E.

4. A: My last name is Davis.
   B: How do you spell it?
   A: D-A-V-I-S.

5. A: I'm Kim.
   B: How do you spell it?
   A: K-I-M.

6. A: My name is Anna.
   B: How do you spell it?
   A: A-N-N-A.

# In Your Experience

**Refer to the general instructions on page x in the Introduction.**

## Preparation

1. Model asking and answering questions about first and last name and spelling names.

2. Ask questions and have students respond with their names and the spelling. Write the names on the board as students spell them.

## Presentation

1. Practice the dialogue: teacher-class, teacher-student, and student-student.

2. Arrange students in pairs and have them practice using their own names.

3. Invite pairs to present their dialogues to the class.

### Page 21

# Sound Bites

**Refer to the general instructions on page ix in the Introduction.**

# Exercise 5

## Preparation

1. Introduce the sight words and ideographs for MEN and WOMEN. Encourage students to comment on where they have seen these signs and symbols.

2. Say the words in random order and have students point to the appropriate sight words and ideographs.

## Presentation

1. Play the tape or read the listening script for the exercise. Have students circle the correct symbols or sight words in their books.

2. Replay the tape and go over the answers with the group.

## Answers to Exercise 5

The following should be circled:

1. ideograph for men
2. ideograph for women
3. ideograph for women
4. ideograph for men
5. MEN
6. WOMEN
7. MEN
8. WOMEN

## Listening Script

1. men
2. women
3. women
4. men
5. men
6. women
7. men
8. women

# Your Turn

**Refer to the general instructions on page x in the Introduction.**

# Exercise 6

## Presentation

1. Have students match the sight words with the symbols or illustrations.

2. Go over the answers with the group.

## Answers to Exercise 6

1. MEN should be matched to the drawing of men and the ideograph of men.

2. WOMEN should be matched to the drawing of women and the ideograph of women.

3. See number two.

4. See number one.

Page 22

# Exercise 7

**Refer to the general instructions on page xii in the Introduction.**

## Preparation

1. Review questions and answers about first and last names.

2. Make a sample form on the board similar to the ones on page 22. Ask students to find the sight words: *Name, First, Last.*

3. Invite a volunteer to come to the board and fill in his or her first and last names in the correct places. You may want to repeat this activity with a different order for the first and last names.

## Presentation

1. Have students look at the exercise on page 22. Review the names of the characters. Ask questions about first and last names of the characters.

2. Ask students to complete the exercise by copying the first and last names of the characters on the forms. Go around the room, helping as needed. Point out the use of an uppercase letter at the beginning of names.

3. Go over the answers. You may want to have volunteers fill out forms on the board for each of the characters.

### Answers to Exercise 7

Box 1: Marc Sedar

Box 2: Sonia Otis

Box 3: Kim Lee

## In Your Experience

Refer to the general instructions on page x in the Introduction.

### Presentation

Elicit or point out to students that they should write their first name before their last (or family) name, even if they traditionally write it differently.

### Page 23

## Sound Bites

Refer to the general instructions on page ix in the Introduction.

## Exercise 8

### Preparation

Write the sight words or display sight word cards on the board: *Name, First, Last.* Ask questions about names and have students point to the sight words used in the questions. For example, say "What's your first name? (first name) What's his name? (name)" Repeat the procedure with sentences about names. Say, "My name is ___. Her last name is ____."

### Presentation

1. Play the tape or read the listening script for the first item. Model how to do the exercise. Tell students they are to circle the word they hear.

2. Continue playing the tape or reading the listening script. Have students circle the word they hear. Replay the tape as needed.

3. Go over the answers with the group.

### Answers to Exercise 8

The following words should be circled:

1. Name      2. First      3. Last

4. Name      5. Last      6. First

### Listening Script

1. What's your name?
2. My first name is Marc.
3. What's your last name?
4. My name is Sonia Otis.
5. My last name is Otis.
6. My first name is Sonia.

## In Your Experience

Refer to the general instructions on page x in the Introduction.

### Preparation

1. Review questions and answers about first and last name.
2. Hold up sight word cards: *Name, First, Last.* Have students respond orally with their own names.

### Presentation

1. Ask students to look at the exercise. Invite volunteers to read aloud the sentences and fill in the missing information about themselves.
2. Tell students to fill in their names in the blanks.
3. Students can draw or tape a photo of themselves in the box under the exercise.
4. In pairs, have students practice reading the sentences about themselves aloud.

### Extension

 **Option:** In mixed-literacy level classes, you may want to give students additional practice with Book 1, Introductory Unit, page viii Vocabulary Prompts.

**Page 24**

## Sound Bites

Refer to the general instructions on page ix in the Introduction.

## Exercise 9

### Preparation

1. Review letters of the alphabet and spelling names.
2. Ask questions about names and spelling names such as, "What's your first name? How do you spell it?" Have students respond appropriately.

### Presentation

1. Write the first item of the exercise on the board. Model the exercise. Play the tape or read the first item from the listening script and demonstrate circling the correct spelling of the name.
2. Have students listen to the rest of the exercise and circle the correct spellings.
3. Go over the answers with the group by asking questions and having students spell the names aloud. Write the names on the board so students can check their work.

## Answers to Exercise 9

The following words should be circled:

1. Ken          2. Lake          3. Peter

4. Nole          5. Han          6. Adams

### Listening Script

1. I'm Ken. K-E-N.

2. My last name is Lake. L-A-K-E.

3. I'm Peter. P-E-T-E-R.

4. My last name is Nole. N-O-L-E.

5. My name's Han. H-A-N.

6. My last name is Adams. A-D-A-M-S.

# Your Turn

Refer to the general instructions on page x in the Introduction.

### Preparation

1. Create a chart on the board by writing the sight words as column headings: *MEN, WOMEN.*

2. Use names of students in the class to demonstrate filling in the chart.

### Presentation

1. Ask students to look at the chart in the book. Go over the example orally. Invite volunteers to read aloud the names of the other characters and to decide which column the names should be written in.

2. Students can work in pairs to complete the chart. Remind students to add their own names to the proper column in the chart.

3. Go over the answers with the group. You may want to make a large class chart on the board as a follow-up activity.

### Extension

 **Option 1:** Write the lines from the conversations in the unit on strips of paper. Students can work in pairs or small groups to arrange the lines in correct order.

**Option 2:** Bring in forms and applications. Have students find the sight words *name, first,* and *last* on the forms. Make copies of the forms and ask students to practice filling in their names in the appropriate places. Students can also practice questions and answers about spelling names, using a chart with the following column headings: *MEN, WOMEN.* Tell students to ask four or five other students in the class for their names. Students should also ask for spelling and then write the names on the chart.

**Option 3:** Introduce and have students practice decoding vowel-consonant and consonant-vowel-consonant combinations. For example: *at (hat, cat, fat, mat); an (pan, can, ran); it (sit, fit); in (pin, tin, win); ot (hot, not, lot).*

### Answers to Your Turn

Names in the chart could include the following:

| WOMEN | MEN |
|---|---|
| Kim Lee | Bill Miller |
| Sonia Otis | Marc Sedar |
| Anna Davis | |

# UNIT 2                                        NUMBERS

## OVERVIEW

### Objectives

#### Skills and Structures

Identify numbers

Respond to information questions about one's phone number

Read phone numbers

Copy/write phone numbers on simple forms

Discriminate among numbers in series

Recognize sight words related to personal information: name, phone number

Count from 1–20

Demonstrate understanding of numerals 11–20

Copy important phone numbers on a chart

#### SCANS Competencies

Foundation Skills

#### Realia

Telephones (real or toy)

Telephone bills

## ACTIVITY NOTES

### Page 25

### Spotlight

**Refer to the general instructions on page xi in the Introduction.**

NOTE: The setup of the following units in the Student Book is similar to that of unit 1. The general procedures for presenting activities would be similar to those presented for unit 1. For the following units, key points to be presented in teaching the unit are highlighted in this guide.

#### Preparation

NOTE: Phone numbers are read as series of single digits. In this unit, 0 is practiced as "zero." Depending on the level of the students, you may want to explain that it is also read as "oh" in phone numbers.

# Sound Bites

Refer to the general instructions on page ix in the Introduction.

## Exercise I

### Presentation

Before reading the numbers, elicit from students that the numbers in the picture are on a telephone.

### Listening Script

One, two, three, four, five, six, seven, eight, nine, zero.

## Page 26

# Your Turn

Refer to the general instructions on page x in the Introduction.

### Presentation

You may want to do this as a chain activity. Ask a student his or her phone number. After they give it, they must turn and ask the person behind them the same question. Have students go around the room in this way until everyone has asked and answered the question. The last student should ask you the question after giving his or her phone number. Depending on the level of your students and the importance of area codes where they live, you may want to introduce area codes at this time.

### Listening Script

A: What's your phone number?

B: Seven-three-one, four-two-eight-nine.

# Reading for Real

Refer to the general instructions on page xii in the Introduction.

### Preparation

Ask students the following question: "What people or places need you to write your name and phone number?" List the ideas on the board.

## Page 27

# Exercise 2

Refer to the general instructions on page xii in the Introduction.

### Presentation

Remind students to check the order of the numbers carefully.

### Answers to Exercise 2

The following numbers should be circled:

| | | |
|---|---|---|
| 1. 123 | 2. 534 | 3. 748 |
| 4. 963 | 5. 502 | 6. 841 |

# Exercise 3

Refer to the general instructions on page xii in the Introduction.

## Answers to Exercise 3

The following should be matched:

1. Phone Number: <u>234-5521</u>
2. Name: Kim Lee
3. Last Name: Bill <u>Miller</u>
4. First Name: <u>Bill</u> Miller

## Page 28

# Sound Bites

Refer to the general instructions on page ix in the Introduction.

# Exercise 4

## Presentation

Remind students that phone numbers are read in a certain rhythm: three digits, pause, four digits. They should remember to listen for the entire number before circling.

## Answers to Exercise 4

The following phone numbers should be circled:

1. 742-8901
2. 547-9695
3. 321-4474
4. 965-4421
5. 827-3355
6. 378-9110

## Listening Script

1. A: My phone number is seven-four-two, eight-nine-zero-one.

   B: Seven-four-two, eight-nine-zero-one?

   A: Yes. That's right.

2. A: My phone number is five-four-seven, nine-six-nine-five.

   B: Five-four-seven, nine-six-nine-five?

   A: Yes. That's right.

3. A: My phone number is three-two-one, four-four-seven-four.

   B: Three-two-one, four-four-seven-four?

   A: Yes. That's right.

4. A: My phone number is nine-six-five, four-four-two-one.

   B: Nine-six-five, four-four-two-one?

   A: Yes. That's right.

5. A: My phone number is eight-two-seven, three-three-five-five.

   B: Eight-two-seven, three-three-five-five?

   A: Yes. That's right.


6. A: My phone number is three-seven-eight, nine-one-one-zero.

   B: Three-seven-eight, nine-one-one-zero?

   A: Yes. That's right.

# Exercise 5

**Refer to the general instructions on page xii in the Introduction.**

## Presentation

Review with the class how many digits are missing in each phone number before you play the tape.

## Extension

 **Option:** In mixed-literacy level classes, you may want to give students additional practice with Book 1, Introductory Unit, page ix Vocabulary Prompts and Your Turn.

## Answers to Exercise 5

The numbers in boldface should be added:

| | | |
|---|---|---|
| 1. 352 - **4519** | 2. **631** - 6468 | 3. 898 - **0321** |
| 4. 776 - **3455** | 5. **851** - 4357 | 6. 452 - **3061** |

## Listening Script

1. My phone number is three-five-two, four-five-one-nine.

2. My phone number is six-three-one, six-four-six-eight.

3. My phone number is eight-nine-eight, zero-three-two-one.

4. My phone number is seven-seven-six, three-four-five-five.

5. My phone number is eight-five-one, four-three-five-seven.

6. My phone number is four-five-two, three-zero-six-one.

# Person to Person

**Refer to the general instructions on page xii in the Introduction.**

## Presentation

1. After modeling the dialogue with a volunteer, ask students why they think Anna repeated Bill's phone number. Is this a good idea?

2. Remind students to practice the dialogue using their own telephone numbers.

# Sound Bites

Refer to the general instructions on page ix in the Introduction.

## Exercise 6

### Presentation

You may want to play the tape or read the numbers in random order and have students point to them as you read.

### Listening Script

eleven, twelve, thirteen, fourteen, fifteen, sixteen, seventeen, eighteen, nineteen, twenty

## Exercise 7

Refer to the general instructions on page xii in the Introduction.

### Answers to Exercise 7

1. 15          2. 13          3. 16          4. 17          5. 12

### Listening Script

1. Fifteen.          4. Seventeen.          2. Thirteen.          5. Twelve.          3. Sixteen.

# Your Turn

Refer to the general instructions on page x in the Introduction.

## Exercise 8

Refer to the general instructions on page xii in the Introduction.

### Preparation

1. Choose students to count classroom objects aloud.
2. On the board write the names of classroom objects such as chairs, desks, pencils, or students. Choose one student to count how many of an object there is in the classroom aloud. Choose another student to write the number on the board next to the object.

### Answers to Exercise 8

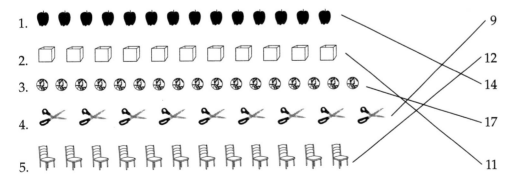

## Exercise 9

**Refer to the general instructions on page xii in the Introduction.**

### Presentation

1. Point out to students that this exercise has four parts. The first set of numbers 1–20 is there for reference only. Read them aloud; then have volunteers do the same.

2. The second and third sets of numbers are there for students to fill in. After students have done them individually, review the correct answers with the class.

3. The final part asks students to count the objects in the pictures and write the number themselves. Again, after students complete this individually, review the correct answers with the class.

### Answers to Exercise 9

The numbers in boldface should be added:
1 **2** 3 **4 5 6** 7 **8 9** 10

**11** 12 13 **14** 15 **16** 17 18 **19 20**

1 **2** 3 **4 5 6 7 8 9** 10

11 **12 13 14 15 16 17 18** 19 20

|        |        |        |
|--------|--------|--------|
| 1. 13  | 2. 16  | 3. 19  |
| 4. 10  | 5. 15  | 6. 12  |

## Sound Bites

**Refer to the general instructions on page ix in the Introduction.**

## Exercise 10

### Presentation

Point out to students that each person will only have one phone number and that the numbers are only used once.

### Answers to Exercise 10

|                  |                  |                  |
|------------------|------------------|------------------|
| 1. 448-9595      | 2. 384-7210      | 3. 912-7792      |
| 4. 212-6764      | 5. 346-4908      |                  |

### Listening Script

1. Sonia's phone number is four-four-eight, nine-five-nine-five.

2. Marc's phone number is three-eight-four, seven-two-one-zero.

3. Bill's phone number is nine-one-two, seven-seven-nine-two.

4. Anna's phone number is two-one-two, six-seven-six-four.

5. Kim's phone number is three-four-six, four-nine-zero-eight.

## In Your Experience

Refer to the general instructions on page x in the Introduction.

### Presentation

Point out that this form, like many others, asks for last name first.

## Page 32

## Sound Bites

Refer to the general instructions on page ix in the Introduction.

## Exercise 11

### Preparation

Tell students they will have to listen for a number within a sentence, not just by itself.

### Answers to Exercise 11

The following numbers should be circled:

| 1. 13 | 2. 14 | 3. 17 | 4. 19 | 5. 12 | 6. 16 |

### Listening Script

1. I have thirteen pencils.
2. She has fourteen papers.
3. I have seventeen books.
4. We have nineteen chairs.
5. You have twelve boxes.
6. He has sixteen apples.

## In Your Experience

Refer to the general instructions on page x in the Introduction.

### Preparation

1. Introduce the symbols and phone numbers of emergency services.
2. Bring in copies of local phone books and help students locate the emergency phone numbers at the front of the books. Encourage students to suggest situations when it would be necessary to call each of the emergency numbers.

### Presentation

If possible, ask students about experiences they have had or have heard about calling for emergency help. Find out if there are bilingual operators at the various emergency numbers. Students can practice calling for help or asking for a bilingual operator to report an emergency in class. Remind them not to call those numbers to practice; call only in case of a real emergency.

### Extension

Students can make their own class phone directory. Give each student a list of people in the class. Tell students to go around the room asking for one another's phone numbers. Students can record the phone numbers next to the appropriate names on the list. Encourage students to call each other to find out about classes they have missed, homework, etc.

## OVERVIEW

### Objectives

#### Skills and Structures

Give personal information about one's address

Ask questions about addresses

Read and recognize street signs

Copy/write one's address on simple forms

Read and respond to sight words: *address, number, street, city, state, zip code*

Name classroom objects

Respond to simple classroom commands such as *Open your book. Close the door.*

Name household objects

Complete simple classroom inventory chart

#### SCANS Competencies

Foundation Skills

#### Realia

Maps of local areas

Maps of the United States

## ACTIVITY NOTES

### Page 33

### Spotlight

Refer to the general instructions on page xi in the Introduction.

### Preparation

As students practice saying and reading addresses, point out that house numbers are usually read in groups; for example: 114 = one-fourteen; 2134 = twenty-one thirty-four. If students live in apartments, be sure to have them include their apartment numbers in their addresses.

# Sound Bites

Refer to the general instructions on page ix in the Introduction.

## Exercise 1

### Preparation

Tell students that addresses have at least two parts: a house or building number, and a street name. If someone lives in an apartment, his or her address will include the apartment number.

### Presentation

Remind students to listen for both parts of the address.

### Listening Script

A: What's your address?

B: One-fourteen Pine Street.


A: What's your address?

B: Eight-oh-two Lake Avenue.

**Page 34**

## Your Turn

Refer to the general instructions on page x in the Introduction.

### Presentation

You may want to do this as a chain activity. Ask a student his or her address. After they give it, they must turn and ask the person behind them the same question. Have students go around the room in this way until everyone has asked and answered the question. The last student should ask you the question after giving his or her address. Remind students who live in an apartment to be sure to give the apartment number.

### Listening Script

A: What's your address?

B: One-fourteen Pine Street.

## Reading for Real

Refer to the general instructions on page xii in the Introduction.

### Presentation

1. Read the first form on page 34.
2. Ask students to point to the sight words and numbers as you say them.
3. Read aloud the various parts of the address and have students find the appropriate sight words: *address, number, street, city, state, zip code.*

4. Repeat the procedure with the second form.

5. Help students say their own addresses.

6. Point out the use of uppercase letters. Help students see that city and state always begin with uppercase letters. So does the street name and the following word: *street*, *road*, and so on.

7. Point out the use of two-letter postal abbreviations for state names and that both letters are uppercase.

### Extension

Present a map of the United States. Invite students to locate their home state and any other states they may have lived in. Present the two-letter postal abbreviations for those states.

### Page 35

## Exercise 2

**Refer to the general instructions on page xii in the Introduction.**

### Preparation

1. Review questions and answers about addresses. Say, "What's your address? What street? What city? What state? What's the zip code?" Guide students to give the information from their own addresses. If needed, give students index cards with their addresses for reference.

2. Write the sight words on word cards. Guide students to identify initial letters and sounds for the words. Point out that the *c* in *city* is an exception and has a soft sound.

3. Hold up a word card and ask the appropriate question. Ask volunteers to give the information from their own addresses. Repeat with the other word cards.

4. Use just the word cards and have students respond with the correct information.

### Presentation

1. Write the first line of the visual-discrimination activity on the board. Point to the first word. Ask a volunteer to read the word. Point to the other words in the line and encourage students to point out the word that is the same. Invite a volunteer to come to the board and circle the answer.

2. Students can complete the exercise individually or in pairs.

3. Go over the answers with the group.

### Answers to Exercise 2

The following words should be circled:

1. ADDRESS     2. STREET     3. CITY
4. STATE          5. ZIP CODE   6. NUMBER

# Exercise 3

**Refer to the general instructions on page xii in the Introduction.**

## Preparation

1. Ask, "What's your address?" Encourage students to respond with their complete addresses.
2. Write a volunteer's address on the board. Use the word cards to review the sight words: *address, number, street, city, state, zip code.* Hold up a word card and have students say or point to the appropriate part of the address on the board.

## Presentation

1. Tell students to look at the exercise in the book. Explain that students need to draw a line from the sight words to the parts of the form. Point out the example.
2. Have students work in pairs to complete the exercise.
3. To go over the answers, ask comprehension questions about the form. For example, ask "What is 95124? Is *CA* the city or state?"

## Answers to Exercise 3

The following items should be matched:

Address: 310 Green Street     City: San Jose     Name: Sonia Otis

Street: Green Street     Zip Code: 95124     State: CA

---

**Page 36**

# Sound Bites

**Refer to the general instructions on page ix in the Introduction.**

# Exercise 4

## Presentation

Point out to students that they will be listening for one word in a sentence or question.

## Answers to Exercise 4

The following words should be circled:

1. Address     2. State     3. Name
4. City     5. Street     6. Zip Code

## Listening Script

1. What's your address?     4. What's your city?
2. What's your state?     5. What street do you live on?
3. What's your name?     6. What's your ZIP code?

## Person to Person

Refer to the general instructions on page xii in the Introduction.

### Presentation

1. Model this dialogue with a volunteer.

2. Remind students to practice the dialogue using their own address, city, state, and zip code.

**Page 37**

## Sound Bites

Refer to the general instructions on page ix in the Introduction.

## Exercise 5

### Preparation

1. Introduce the classroom objects by pointing to and saying the words. Have students repeat.

2. Demonstrate actions involving the objects as you say the commands. For example, say "Go to the door. Go to the table. Go to the chair."

3. Make word cards for the objects. Have volunteers attach them to the correct objects.

### Presentation

 **Option 1:** For lower level students say the commands and ask volunteers to go to the correct objects.

**Option 2:** Invite volunteers to give some commands for you or other students to do.

**Option 3:** For more advanced students, introduce and practice additional commands such as the following:

- Open the door.
- Open the book.
- Pick up the pen.
- Put the pen down.
- Stand next to the table.
- Stand next to the chair.

### Listening Script

Window.      Door.      Book.      Table.      Chair.      Pen.

## Exercise 6

Refer to the general instructions on page xii in the Introduction.

### Presentation

1. Play the tape or read the listening script and have students circle the objects they hear in the commands.

2. Replay the cassette to help students check their own work.

3. Go over the answers with the class.

## Answers to Exercise 6

1. door      4. pen
2. window     5. table
3. book

## Listening Script

1. Close the door, please.
2. Open the window.
3. Open your book.
4. Put your pen down.
5. Walk to the table, please.

# Your Turn

Refer to the general instructions on page x in the Introduction.

# Exercise 7

## Answers to Exercise 7

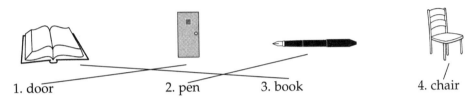

1. door        2. pen        3. book         4. chair

**Page 38**

# Exercise 8

Refer to the general instructions on page xii in the Introduction.

## Presentation

1. Ask students to look at the illustration.
2. Say the names of the objects and have students point to them.
3. Tell students to count the different objects.
4. Students can work in pairs to complete the chart.
5. Go over the answers with the group. NOTE: Depending on students' level, you may want to point out the use of *s* at the end of words to show plural ("more than one").
6. You may want to have the class make its own classroom inventory chart. Ask students to brainstorm items to include on list. Then have them count and complete the chart.

## Answers to Exercise 8

tables: 4, windows: 2, doors: 2, books: 5

**Page 39**

# Sound Bites

Refer to the general instructions on page ix in the Introduction.

# Exercise 9

## Preparation

Write the information about Sonia Otis on the board as it would appear on an envelope. Then review questions and sight words about addresses before having students complete the listening exercise.

## Presentation

1. Play the first item on the tape or read it from the listening script. Be sure students understand the two steps in the exercise: circle the sight word and then match the sight word to the correct information.

2. Replay the tape to help students check their work. Then go over the answers with the group.

## Answers to Exercise 9

1. Name; should be matched to (D) Sonia Otis.
2. Phone; should be matched to (E) 384-7210.
3. Address; should be matched to (A) 520 Park Street.
4. City; should be matched to (B) Denver.
5. Zip code; should be matched to (C) 06321.

## Listening Script

1. What's your name?
2. What's your phone number?
3. What's your address?
4. What's your city?
5. What's your zip code?

# In Your Experience

Refer to the general instructions on page x in the Introduction.

## Preparation

1. Review personal information questions about name, address, and phone numbers.

2. Use word cards to review the sight words. Hold up cards and have students respond with their information.

## Presentation

Tell students to copy or write their personal information on the form. Go around the room. Help students use uppercase letters at the beginning of proper names. Remind students that city and state names begin with an uppercase letter, as does the street name.

## Page 40

# Sound Bites

Refer to the general instructions on page ix in the Introduction.

# Exercise 10

## Presentation

Point out to students that they will be circling the answers to questions they hear. Model the first question for students so they understand.

## Answers to Exercise 10

The following items should be circled:

1. 818 South Street
2. Somerville
3. MA
4. 713-6214
5. 04756
6. Kim Lee

## Listening Script

1. What's her address?
2. What's her city?
3. What's her state?
4. What's his phone number?
5. What's the zip code?
6. What's her name?

# Your Turn

**Refer to the general instructions on page x in the Introduction.**

## Presentation

1. Have students practice asking and answers questions about addresses.

2. Make a chart on the board similar to the one in the book.

3. Model asking a volunteer his or her address. Demonstrate writing the volunteer's name and address in the appropriate columns of the chart. Repeat with other students if needed.

4. Invite students to ask three others for their addresses and to record them on the chart. Encourage students to ask for clarification by repeating information and asking for spelling. Go around the room listening and helping as needed.

## Extension

1. Have the group take a walking tour of the neighborhood. Encourage students to point out house or building numbers and street names. Then invite students to say the addresses of places in the neighborhood.

2. Bring in a map of the local area. Students can look for their towns and streets on the map. You may also want to bring in a map of the United States. Have students point out states that they know or where they lived. Introduce abbreviations for the states that students know.

3. Demonstrate addressing an envelope. Then give students envelopes. Students can write their own addresses for the return address and then address the envelope to a friend.

   **Option:** More advanced students can practice initial consonant clusters such as *st, dr, str.* Use words such as the following:

   - *st* (stop, state, step, stand, still)
   - *dr* (drive, drop, drill, drag)
   - *str* (street, stress, strap)

4. Use words from the unit to practice decoding skills. Divide multisyllable words into syllables for students to read. You may want to write the syllables of target words on separate cards. As you say the words, have students find the correct cards to form the words. Some words to use might be *ad-dress, num-ber, a-part-ment,* and *win-dow.*

# LEFT OR RIGHT?

## OVERVIEW

### Objectives

#### Skills and Structures

Ask and answer questions about location of buildings

Identify places in the community

Express gratitude

Discriminate between left and right

Ask questions with *where*

Recognize place names in signs

Copy place names

Count from 1–30

Recognize numerals 1–30

Recognize addresses

#### SCANS Competencies

Foundation Skills

#### Realia

Dollar bills and coins

Bank deposit slip

Check

Food

Grocery store ads

Postmarked letter and stamps

Library books

Library card

Telephone books

Local street maps

## ACTIVITY NOTES

### Page 41

### Spotlight

**Refer to the general instructions on page xi in the Introduction.**
NOTE: Discuss how body language can be useful in giving and understanding directions. Use local street names and maps in the exercises so students can become more familiar with their local areas. Throughout the unit encourage students to point as they give directions.

## Preparation

1. Introduce names of places in the community. Show pictures or items associated with the various places. For example: money, deposit slip, check (bank); food and advertisements (grocery store); letters and stamps (post office); library books and library card (library). Encourage students to talk about places they visit and what they do in each of the places.

2. Hold up pictures of each of the places and model the place names. Have students repeat.

3. Say place names and have students point to pictures of the places or act out what they do in the places.

## Sound Bites

Refer to the general instructions on page ix in the Introduction.

## Exercise 1

### Listening Script

Store.       Bank.       Library.       Post office.

**Page 42**

## Your Turn

Refer to the general instructions on page x in the Introduction.

### Preparation

Write the place names on the board along with the local street they are on. Review this information with the class. Focus on clear pronunciation of the locations and street names. Tell students to use this information when they practice the activity.

### Extension

 Option: In mixed-literacy level classes, you may want to give students additional practice with Book 1, Unit 6, Reading for Real, page 55.

### Listening Script

A: Where's the bank?

B: It's on Green Street.

A: Thanks.

B: You're welcome.

## Reading for Real

Refer to the general instructions on page xii in the Introduction.

### Preparation

1. Draw two arrows on the board, one pointing left and one pointing right. Model the words *left* and *right*.

2. Say the words again, pointing in the directions. Ask students to repeat and also point in the directions as they say them. It's a good idea to turn toward the board slightly so that you are looking at the arrows from the same viewpoint as the class.

3. Say *left* and *right* in random order and have students point in the correct directions.

4. Point to the arrows on the board in random order and ask students to give the direction words.

5. Write the words on the board. Guide students to notice the initial letters and number of letters in each of the words. Encourage students to discuss where they have seen the words *left* and *right*.

## Presentation

1. Tell students to look at the illustration. Ask students to identify the street and places in the illustration.

2. Read aloud the text. Have students find and point to the words *left* and *right* in the reading. Ask students to find other words they know in the reading.

3. Read the text again and encourage students to read aloud with you. Ask simple comprehension questions. For example, say "Is the store on Green Street? Is the post office on Main Street? Is the store on the left or right?"

4. Arrange students in pairs and have them practice reading the text together.

## Page 43

# Exercise 2

**Refer to the general instructions on page xii in the Introduction.**

## Presentation

Tell students they should circle only the word that matches exactly.

### Answers to Exercise 2

The following words should be circled:

1. BANK
2. STORE
3. POST OFFICE
4. LIBRARY
5. HOSPITAL
6. SCHOOL

# Exercise 3

**Refer to the general instructions on page xii in the Introduction.**

## Preparation

Review the content of the pictures with the class. Answer any questions students may have.

### Answers to Exercise 3

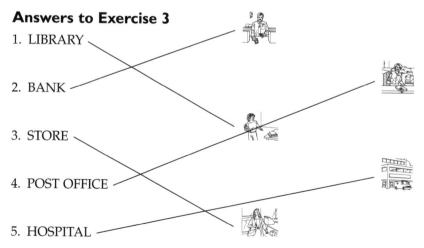

1. LIBRARY
2. BANK
3. STORE
4. POST OFFICE
5. HOSPITAL

# Sound Bites

Refer to the general instructions on page ix in the Introduction.

# Exercise 4

## Preparation

1. Draw a street going vertically down the board. You may want to draw left and right arrows on the appropriate sides.

2. Hold up a picture of a bank. Say, "The bank is on the right." Tape or attach the picture of the bank on the right side of the road.

3. Repeat the procedure with other places. Encourage volunteers to attach the pictures on the correct sides of the road.

4. Remove the pictures. Draw several squares on each side of the street. Repeat the exercise but have students copy or write the place names in the appropriate squares on the board.

## Presentation

1. Tell students to look at the exercise in the book. Ask a volunteer to read aloud the place names in the first column. Explain that students will hear a sentence about each of the places. Point out that students need to write the place name on the left or right side of the street.

2. Play the tape or read the listening script. Replay as needed.

3. Go over the answers with the group.

4. Ask *where* questions about the exercise and have students respond with the correct direction words.

## Answers to Exercise 4

The two squares on the left should be labeled *store* and *hospital*. The two squares on the right should be labeled *bank* and *library*.

## Listening Script

1. A: Where's the bank?
   B: It's on the right.

2. A: Where's the store?
   B: It's on the left.

3. A: Where's the hospital?
   B: It's on the left.

4. A: Where's the library?
   B: It's on the right.

# Your Turn

Refer to the general instructions on page x in the Introduction.

## Presentation

Remind students to use the map from Exercise 4 to answer their partners' questions.

## Sound Bites

Refer to the general instructions on page ix in the Introduction.

# Exercise 5

### Presentation

After students listen the first time, you may want to play the tape again or read the numbers in random order and have students point to the numbers as you say them.

### Listening Script

One, two, three, four, five.

Six, seven, eight, nine, ten.

Eleven, twelve, thirteen, fourteen, fifteen.

Sixteen, seventeen, eighteen, nineteen, twenty.

Twenty-one, twenty-two, twenty-three, twenty-four, twenty-five.

Twenty-six, twenty-seven, twenty-eight, twenty-nine, thirty.

# Exercise 6

Refer to the general instructions on page xii in the Introduction.

### Answers to Exercise 6

The following numbers should be circled:

1. 27          2. 29          3. 24          4. 18          5. 26

### Listening Script

1. Twenty-seven. 2. Twenty-nine. 3. Twenty-four. 4. Eighteen. 5. Twenty-six.

## Your Turn

Refer to the general instructions on page x in the Introduction.

# Exercise 7

### Answers to Exercise 7

1. 18          2. 28          3. 21          4. 20

# Exercise 8

Refer to the general instructions on page xii in the Introduction.

### Presentation

1. Point out to students that this exercise has two parts. Elicit from students that in the first part they should write the missing numbers in order from 1–30.

2. Explain that the second part of the exercise is a list of room numbers on either side of a hall. Students are to fill in the missing numbers in order.

## Answers to Exercise 8

The numbers in boldface should be added.

|   | 1 | 2 | 3 | **4** | **5** | 6 |
|---|---|---|---|---|---|---|
| **7** | **8** | 9 | 10 | **11** | **12** | **13** |
| **14** | **15** | **16** | **17** | **18** | **19** | 20 |
| 21 | **22** | **23** | **24** | 25 | **26** | **27** |
| **28** | **29** | 30 | | | | |

Room 21          Room 22

Room 23          Room **24**

Room **25**          Room **26**

Room **27**          Room **28**

Room **29**          Room 30

## Page 47

# Sound Bites

**Refer to the general instructions on page ix in the Introduction.**

# Exercise 9

## Preparation

Review each picture with the class and answer any questions they may have before proceeding.

## Answers to Exercise 9

The following pictures should be circled:

1. post office     4. store
2. hospital        5. bank
3. library

## Listening Script

1. A: Where's the post office?
   B: It's on the right.

2. A: Where's the hospital?
   B: It's on the left.

3. A: Where's the library?
   B: It's on Green Street.

4. A: Where's the store?
   B: It's on River Road.

5. A: Where's the bank?
   B: It's on Main Street.

## Your Turn

Refer to the general instructions on page x in the Introduction.

### Preparation

1. Ask a volunteer to read aloud the words in the box. Alternatively, say the words in random order and have students point to them.
2. Have students name the places and describe the locations of the places in the illustration. If needed, use questions to guide students.

### Presentation

1. Write the first sentence of the cloze exercise on the board. Demonstrate filling in first blank with one of the words from the box.
2. Depending on students' level, you may want to read aloud the paragraph before students fill in the blanks or have them complete the exercise on their own.
3. Go over the answers with the group. Ask questions about the selection to check comprehension.

### Answers to Your Turn

The post___**office**___is on Green Street. It's on the___**right**___. The store is on **Green**___Street. It's on the___**left**___. The___**bank**___is on Green___**Street**___. It's on the left.

## Page 48

## Sound Bites

Refer to the general instructions on page ix in the Introduction.

## Exercise 10

### Presentation

Tell students they will hear both a question and an answer for each location.

### Answers to Exercise 10

The following addresses should be circled:

1. 28 Main Street  2. 324 Green Street  3. 722 River Road  4. 520 Adams Avenue
5. 623 Hope Drive

### Listening Script

1. A: Where's the post office?

   B: It's at twenty-eight Main Street.

2. A: Where's the library?

   B: It's at three-twenty-four Green Street.

3. A: Where's the hospital?

   B: It's at seven twenty-two River Road.

4. A: Where's the bank?

   B: It's at five-twenty Adams Avenue.

5. A: Where's the school?

   B: It's at six twenty-three Hope Drive.

# In Your Experience

**Refer to the general instructions on page x in the Introduction.**

## Preparation

1. Bring in realia from various places in the community. Help students identify the places associated with the items. For example: stamps, change of address form, aerogram = post office.

2. Ask students where the places are located in their communities. You may want to bring in copies of local phone books and Yellow Pages or have the class take a walk through the community to notice places and addresses. Help students find the addresses and phone numbers of places they know in the community.

## Presentation

1. Have students fill in the addresses and phone numbers in the chart. Students can choose an additional place to add to the chart.

2. Arrange students in pairs and have them practice asking and answering questions about the locations and phone numbers of the places on their charts.

## Extension

1. Have groups of students make a map of the neighborhood on a large piece of paper. Help students draw and label local streets and place buildings on the map. Use the map for practice in asking and answering questions about locations and directions.

2. Use chairs and tables to create a maze in the classroom. Introduce it to students and have them practice simple directions. For example, say the following: "Go two steps. Turn left. Go three steps. Turn right." Give directions and have volunteers go through the maze. Have the class give you directions to go through the maze. You may want to change the maze several times. To make the activity more challenging, blindfold a volunteer and have the others give directions to guide the student through the maze.

3. Bring in local street maps. Have students find streets they know. Point out and discuss abbreviations used for streets, such as the following:

   - Ave. (Avenue)
   - St. (Street)
   - Rd. (Road)
   - Dr. (Drive)
   - Blvd. (Boulevard)
   - Pkwy. (Parkway)

4. Reinforce numbers by having students find numbers in different real-life reading materials. For example: calendar pages, pages of a book, room numbers, building directories, TV programs, newspapers, etc.

5. Play number games with dice. Students can roll the dice and then add or multiply the numbers on the dice.

6. Use words from the unit for decoding final consonant clusters: *bank, left,* and *post.* You may want to exaggerate the pronunciation of the consonants to make sure students hear the sounds. NOTE: Final consonants can cause students difficulty and frequently students omit them. Reinforce their pronunciation. Some additional words for practice of final consonant clusters are the following: *nd (end, send, bend, lend, and, hand, land, band)* and *st (post, most, host).*

## OVERVIEW

### Objectives

#### Skills and Structures

Demonstrate understanding of hourly times on analog and digital clocks

Ask and answer questions about time

Express gratitude

Read opening and closing times on signs

Write hourly times

Count from 1-60

Identify hourly times associated with daily activities

Discriminate between A.M. and P.M.

#### SCANS Competencies

Foundation Skills

#### Realia

An analog clock with movable hands

A bus schedule

A TV schedule

A movie schedule

A school schedule

## ACTIVITY NOTES

### Page 49

### Spotlight

**Refer to the general instructions on page xi in the Introduction.**

#### Preparation

1. Introduce hourly times in this unit using an analog clock with movable hands. Move the clock hands to show the time: *1:00.* Say, "It's one o'clock." Have students repeat.

2. Show and say other times for students to repeat.

3. Say a time and have volunteers move the hands of the clock to show the correct time.

4. Show times on the clock and ask students to say the times.

#### Presentation

Tell students to look at the clocks in the illustration. Encourage students to talk about the times shown on the clocks.

## Sound Bites

Refer to the general instructions on page ix in the Introduction.

## Exercise 1

### Preparation

1. Show 2:00 on the analog clock. Model a question and answer in the following way: "What time is it? It's two o'clock." Have students repeat.

2. Show other times and ask, "What time is it?" Have the class give the answers.

### Presentation

1. Play the tape or read the listening script. You may want to have students just listen first. Replay the tape and have students repeat the questions and answers.

2. Practice the question and answers without the cassette. Invite volunteers to ask the questions and have other students give the answers.

### Listening Script

One o'clock.          Five o'clock.          Seven o'clock.          Ten o'clock.

## Exercise 2

Refer to the general instructions on page xii in the Introduction.

### Presentation

1. Tell students they will hear both a question and an answer.

2. Have the class and individual students repeat the question before you play or read the answer.

### Listening Script

A: What time is it?

B: It's five o'clock.

### Page 50

## Your Turn

Refer to the general instructions on page x in the Introduction.

### Preparation

With the class review the times shown in the analog clocks at the end of Your Turn.

### Presentation

After students have repeated the dialogue, elicit or explain the meaning of the use of "Excuse me."

### Listening Script

A: Excuse me. What time is it?

B: It's ten o'clock.

A: Thanks.

B: You're welcome.

## Reading for Real

**Refer to the general instructions on page xii in the Introduction.**

### Preparation

1. Have students look at the first sign in the reading exercise. Tell students to point to and read the times. Ask students to find the word *store.* You may want to have students circle the times' names on the sign.

2. Read aloud the first sign as students follow along in their books. Ask a volunteer to show the times on the analog clock.

3. Repeat the procedure for the second sign. If students ask, explain the days that are included on the sign, but do not spend a lot of time on the days of the week.

4. Write on the board: *OPEN, CLOSED.* Guide students to identify the letters in the words. Help students decode the words. Invite volunteers to explain the words.

### Presentation

Reread the signs as students read aloud with you. You may want to ask simple comprehension questions about the signs such as the following: "Does the store open at 7:00 or 9:00? What time does the bank close?"

### Extension

 **Option:** In mixed-literacy level classes, you may want to give students additional practice with Book 1, Introductory Unit, page xii.

### Page 51

## Exercise 3

**Refer to the general instructions on page xii in the Introduction.**

### Answers to Exercise 3

The following times should be circled:

1. 7:00         2. 2:00         3. 12:00         4. 8:00

## Exercise 4

**Refer to the general instructions on page xii in the Introduction.**

### Answers to Exercise 4

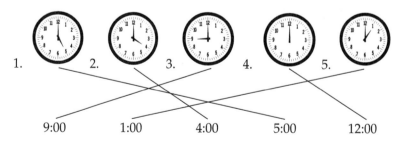

## Your Turn

Refer to the general instructions on page x in the Introduction.

## Exercise 5

### Preparation

On the board write the words *bank, store,* and *library.* With the class have students guess when they think a bank, store, and library might open and close. Write their ideas on the board under the appropriate heading. When students have completed the exercise, review the correct answers with the class. Check how accurate the guesses were.

### Answers to Exercise 5

| BANK | STORE | Wilson Library |
|---|---|---|
| OPEN: 9:00 | OPEN: 7:00 | OPEN: 1:00 |
| CLOSED: 6:00 | CLOSED: 12:00 | CLOSED: 5:00 |

## Person to Person

Refer to the general instructions on page xii in the Introduction.

### Extension

For additional practice, model a dialogue asking what time the bank closes. Have students practice using the closing times for the other locations.

### Listening Script

A: What time does the bank open?

B: Nine o'clock.

A: Thank you.

B: You're welcome.

## Reading for Real

Refer to the general instructions on page xii in the Introduction.

### Presentation

Elicit from students that the sign is posting hours for two different places, a post office and a library.

### Answers to Reading for Real

1. 8:00          2. 10:00          3. 5:00          4. 7:00

# Spotlight

Refer to the general instructions on page xi in the Introduction.

## Presentation

To practice numbers, have a number bee. Divide the class into two teams and have them stand in a line near the board. Say a number and have a team member write the following number on the board. Alternate giving numbers to teams. If a student can't write the number in five seconds, he or she must sit down. The last team with a member standing wins.

# Sound Bites

Refer to the general instructions on page ix in the Introduction.

# Exercise 6

## Presentation

Point out that students only have three choices for each number.

## Answers to Exercise 6

| | | |
|---|---|---|
| 1. 34 | 4. 45 | 7. 53 |
| 2. 60 | 5. 38 | 8. 15 |
| 3. 39 | 6. 40 | |

## Listening Script

| | |
|---|---|
| 1. Thirty-four. | 5. Thirty-eight. |
| 2. Sixty. | 6. Forty. |
| 3. Thirty-nine. | 7. Fifty-three. |
| 4. Forty-five. | 8. Fifteen. |

# Exercise 7

Refer to the general instructions on page xii in the Introduction.

## Presentation

Remind students to write numerals. They should not try to spell out the numbers.

## Answers to Exercise 7

1. 36    2. 52    3. 45    4. 60    5. 48    6. 33

## Listening Script

1. Thirty-six. 2. Fifty-two. 3. Forty-five. 4. Sixty. 5. Forty-eight. 6. Thirty-three.

# Your Turn

Refer to the general instructions on page x in the Introduction.

## Presentation

Elicit from students that the numbers they need to fill in should be in order.

## Answers to Your Turn

The numbers in boldface should be added:

1. 31 **32** 33 34 **35**
2. 46 47 **48** 49 **50**
3. 54 **55** 56 **57** 58

**Page 55**

## Sound Bites

**Refer to the general instructions on page ix in the Introduction.**

## Exercise 8

### Extension

After students have completed the listening activity, they can role-play asking and answering questions about opening and closing times of the places in the activity.

### Answers to Exercise 8

1. Open: 8:00; Closed: 4:00
2. Open: 11:00; Closed 8:00
3. Open: 7:00; Closed 7:00
4. Open: 9:00; Closed 6:00

### Listening Script

1. A: What time does the bank open?
   B: Eight o'clock.
   A: What time does the bank close?
   B: Four o'clock.

2. A: What time does the library open?
   B: Eleven o'clock.
   A: What time does the library close?
   B: Eight o'clock.

3. A: What time does the post office open?
   B: Seven o'clock.
   A: What time does the post office close?
   B: Seven o'clock.

4. A: What time does the store open?
   B: Nine o'clock.
   A: What time does the store close?
   B: Six o'clock.

# In Your Experience

Refer to the general instructions on page x in the Introduction.

## Preparation

1. Mime actions for daily activities. Show the times for the activities on the analog clock. For example: wake up = 7:00, eat = 12:00, class = 6:00.

2. Encourage students to indicate times when they do the various activities. For more advanced students, you may want to introduce vocabulary for the activities.

## Presentation

1. Have students look at the pictures and write the times when they do the activities.

2. As a group, compare and talk about the daily schedules. Students can talk about other routine activities and times.

## Answers to In Your Experience

Answers will vary. Here are some possible answers:

1. 7:00 A.M.     3. 2:00 P.M.     5. 8:00 A.M.

2. 6:00 P.M.     4. 8:00 P.M.     6. 6:30 P.M.

# Culture Corner

Refer to the general instructions on page xiii in the Introduction.

## Presentation

1. Ask students to look at the illustrations. Invite a volunteer to read the times.

2. Point out the abbreviations A.M. and P.M. Encourage students to suggest what A.M. and P.M. might mean. If needed, go through the times with the analog clock to show when A.M. ends and P.M. begins.

3. Have students look back at the previous exercise, and ask students if the times are A.M. or P.M. Students can fill in the A.M./P.M. for their daily activities.

4. As a group compare the A.M./P.M.. times with time systems used in students' native countries. In some countries, times are given in terms of 24 hours. For example: 6:00 = 6:00 A.M., 18:00 = 6:00 P.M.

## Extension

1. Write digital times on one set of cards and analog clocks with the times on another set. Have students use the sets of cards to play matching games and to practice questions and answers about times.

2. Ask students to find and copy opening and closing times of various buildings and businesses in the area. Have students share their findings with the class.

3. Have students look back at the chart of addresses and phone numbers of places in Unit 4 on page 48. Role-play calling and asking for information about opening and closing times. Then encourage students to actually call and ask when a place is open.

# UNIT 6                                   MY FAMILY

## OVERVIEW

### Objectives

#### Skills and Structures

Identify family members by name, age, and relationship

Demonstrate understanding of family relationship terms

Recognize sight words: *age, relationship, children, son, daughter, wife, husband, family*

Write/copy basic information about family

Ask and answer questions about age

Ask and answer yes/no questions with the verb *to be*

Count and write numbers 1–100

Discriminate among titles: *Mr., Ms., Mrs., Miss*

#### SCANS Competencies

Foundation Skills

#### Realia

Forms asking for information about one's family (for students to fill in).

## ACTIVITY NOTES

### Page 57

### Spotlight

**Refer to the general instructions on page xi in the Introduction.**

NOTE: Family may be a sensitive issue. Some students may have lost family members or be separated from their families. Students may or may not want to discuss families. Provide students with language they need to talk about their particular situations.

### Sound Bites

**Refer to the general instructions on page ix in the Introduction.**

### Exercise I

#### Listening Script

Family.          Father.          Mother.          Son.          Daughter.

# Exercise 2

**Refer to the general instructions on page ix in the Introduction.**

## Presentation

Tell students to listen as you play or read the whole dialogue. Then play or read the dialogue one line at a time. Have the class repeat each line. Then play the whole dialogue again and have the class repeat the whole dialogue.

## Listening Script

A: Here's a picture of my family.

B: Oh. Who's that?

A: That's my daughter. Her name is Mary.

## Page 58

# Your Turn

**Refer to the general instructions on page x in the Introduction.**

## Preparation

1. In this dialogue students will need to use the possessive adjectives *his* and *her*. Model questions and answers about students' names such as the following: "What's his name? His name is Miguel. What's her name? Her name is Hung." Guide students to understand that *his* is used for men and *her* is used for women.

2. Contracted forms are commonly used in conversation. Introduce and practice them as single units. If students ask, show how the two words are contracted.

## Presentation

Have students draw or bring photographs of their family to use in this activity.

## Extension

 **Option:** In mixed-literacy level classes, you may want to give students additional practice with Book 1, Unit 1 Vocabulary Prompts page 2, and Culture Corner page 6.

## Listening Script

A: This is my family.

B: Who's that?

A: That's my daughter. Her name is Mary.

# Reading for Real

**Refer to the general instructions on page xii in the Introduction.**

## Preparation

With the class ask students who they would need to give this information to.

## Exercise 3

Refer to the general instructions on page xii in the Introduction.

### Answers to Exercise 3

The following words should be circled:

1. CHILDREN    2. HUSBAND    3. WIFE    4. SON    5. DAUGHTER

## Exercise 4

Refer to the general instructions on page xii in the Introduction.

### Answers to Exercise 4

1. third picture  2. fifth picture  3. second picture  4. first picture  5. sixth picture

6. fourth picture

# In Your Experience

Refer to the general instructions on page x in the Introduction.

### Preparation

1. Introduce relationship terms for extended families as needed; here are some examples: *cousin, uncle, grandparents.*

2. Last-name conventions vary from culture to culture. Members of one family may have different last names.

### Presentation

Students can draw or attach a photo of their families in the top box and then copy or write information about the family members in the form below.

### Extension

 **Option:** In mixed-literacy level classes, you may want to give students additional practice with Book 1, Unit 1 Your Turn page 6.

# Person to Person

Refer to the general instructions on page xii in the Introduction.

### Preparation

Students will be using the subject pronouns *he* and *she*. Model questions and answers about students' ages. For example, say "How old is Miguel? He's 30. How old is Marta? She's 26." Guide students to understand that *he* is used to refer to a man or boy and *she* is used for a woman or girl.

## Presentation

After students have practiced the dialogue, tell them to talk about their own families using the family information form they filled out on page 60.

## Listening Script

A: Is this your brother?

B: Yes, it is.

A: How old is he?

B: He's 22.

# Reading for Real

Refer to the general instructions on page xii in the Introduction.

## Presentation

Remind students to use the information in the form to answer the questions.

## Extension

**Option:** In mixed-literacy level classes, you may want to give students additional practice with Book 1, Unit 1 Exercise 5 page 6.

## Answers to Reading for Real

1. Raymond Sedar      2. Marie Sedar      3. 15      4. 17

Page 62

# Spotlight

Refer to the general instructions on page xi in the Introduction.

## Presentation

Elicit from students that numbers have been skipped. Ask individual students to tell the class what numbers are in between 40 and 50, for example.

# Sound Bites

Refer to the general instructions on page ix in the Introduction.

# Exercise 5

## Answers to Exercise 5

| | | | |
|---|---|---|---|
| 1. 70 | 2. 45 | 3. 28 | 4. 31 |
| 5. 82 | 6. 76 | 7. 65 | 8. 91 |

### Listening Script

1. He's seventy.
2. She's forty-five.
3. I'm twenty-eight.
4. He's thirty-one.
5. She's eighty-two.
6. He's seventy-six.
7. Is he sixty-five?
8. Is she ninety-one?

## Exercise 6

Refer to the general instructions on page xii in the Introduction.

### Answers to Exercise 6

1. 77
2. 62
3. 95
4. 83
5. 54
6. 39

### Listening Script

1. Seventy-seven.
2. Sixty-two.
3. Ninety-five.
4. Eighty-three.
5. Fifty-four.
6. Thirty-nine.

## Your Turn

Refer to the general instructions on page x in the Introduction.

### Extension

Bring in lists of addresses of places in the neighborhood, such as stores and banks. Have students work in pairs to read the addresses. Remind students how to group numbers for reading addresses.

### Answers to Your Turn

The numbers in boldface should be added:

81 **82 83** 84 **85 86 87**

75 76 **77 78** 79 **80** 81

10 20 **30** 40 **50** 60 **70 80 90** 100

**Page 63**

## Sound Bites

Refer to the general instructions on page ix in the Introduction.

## Exercise 7

### Preparation

Review the family information form with students. Point out that each person has two ages listed, and they should circle the one they hear.

### Answers to Exercise 7

The following terms and numbers should be circled:

Bill Miller, 44

Susan Miller, wife, 42

David Miller, son, 16

Linda Miller, daughter, 12

**Listening Script**

A: What's your name?

B: Bill Miller.

A: How old are you?

B: I'm forty-four.

A: Are you married?

B: Yes.

A: What's your wife's name?

B: Susan Miller.

A: How old is she?

B: She's forty-two.

A: Do you have any children?

B: Yes, two children. My son's name is David, and my daughter's name is Linda.

A: How old are they?

B: David is sixteen and Linda is twelve.

## Pages 63-64

# Your Turn

**Refer to the general instructions on page x in the Introduction.**

## Preparation

1. Show a picture of a man. Model the dialogue in the example.
2. Repeat the dialogue line by line. Have students repeat each line.
3. Repeat the procedure with a picture of a woman. Model the dialogue substituting *she* for *he* and a woman's name.
4. Invite pairs of students to say the dialogue.
5. Write on the board: *Name _____, Age _____.*
6. Model the information-gap exercise. Point to a student and ask: "Who is that? How old is he/she?" Encourage others to answer. Write the information on the board. Repeat as needed.

## Presentation

1. Arrange students into groups A and B.
2. Tell Group A to look at the illustrations on page 63 and practice asking questions about the two people. Explain that they will ask questions and then write the names and ages under the illustrations.
3. Tell Group B to look at the illustrations on page 64. Help them read the names and ages of the two people. Explain that they will give the information to their partners.
4. Pair students from A with students from B. A will ask questions and B will respond.

5. Invite pairs to present the questions and answers to the class. Write the names and ages on the board for students to check their work.

6. Have students go back to the groups A and B. Tell Group B to practice questions about name and age for the next part of the exercise. Group A should practice giving the names and ages of the people at the bottom of page 63.

7. Pair students from A with students from B again and have them complete the second part of the information gap.

8. Invite pairs to present the questions and answers to the class. Write the names and ages on the board for students to check their work.

**Answers to Your Turn**

*Student A*

Name: Bill

Age: 28

Name: Judy

Age: 30

*Student B*

Name: David

Age: 32

Name: Ellen

Age: 29

**Page 64**

# Culture Corner

**Refer to the general instructions on page xiii in the Introduction.**

## Presentation

After presenting the titles, have students write the names of their own family members with titles. Explain that children usually do not have titles used with their names and that married women can choose to have the titles of *Mrs.* or *Ms.* Single women may use the titles *Miss* or *Ms.* Introduce other titles as needed.

## Extension

1. Bring in forms that require information about family, such as school, health care, insurance, or social service forms. Ask students if they have seen or filled out these forms. Have students find sections about family members. Ask them to point to or circle sight words: *age, relationship*, etc. If possible, make copies of the forms for students to practice filling out family information.

2. Introduce additional family relationship and marital-status terms such as the following: *cousin, uncle, aunt, grandfather, grandmother; married, single, divorced, widowed, separated.* Help students describe their own family situations and record the information on simplified forms.

3. Have students make a set of word cards for the sight words *name, address, phone number,* and *age.* On another set, have them write their own personal information. Have students match the sight words with the personal information. As an alternative, have students use the personal information for family members and include the sight word *relationship.*

4. Introduce and practice consonant digraphs *ch, th,* and *sh.* Model the sounds and practice them in words from this unit: *ch (children); th (brother, mother, father, this, that, three; sh (she, shop, relationship).*

## OVERVIEW

### Objectives

#### Skills and Structures

Demonstrate understanding of common job titles

Respond to questions about one's occupation

Recognize job titles on help wanted ads

Fill out a simple job information form

Answer simple questions about one's work experience

Demonstrate understanding of years (dates)

Write years

Ask simple questions

Recognize common safety signs with words and symbols

#### SCANS Competencies

Foundation Skills

#### Realia

International warning or danger signs, including ones for no smoking, poison, high voltage, fire alarm, fire extinguisher

Job applications and want ads

## ACTIVITY NOTES

### Page 65

### Spotlight

Refer to the general instructions on page xi in the Introduction.

### Preparation

Encourage students to talk about the bulletin board. Ask if they have ever seen help-wanted ads and if so, where they have seen them. Students can discuss where they can look for jobs or who they can talk to about jobs. Invite students to share experiences they have had or friends have had looking for jobs. Discussion can be in students' native languages.

### Sound Bites

Refer to the general instructions on page ix in the Introduction.

# Exercise 1

## Preparation

Tell students they will hear the names of the jobs on the bulletin board.

## Listening Script

Cashier.     Driver.     Cook.     Dishwasher.     Painter.

# Exercise 2

**Refer to the general instructions on page xii in the Introduction.**

## Preparation

Students should practice talking about their own past or present jobs. Introduce names of jobs that students have had in the past or that they currently have.

## Presentation

Tell students to listen as you play or read the whole dialogue. Then play or read the dialogue one line at a time. Have the class repeat each line. Then play the whole dialogue again and have the class repeat the whole dialogue.

## Listening Script

A: I need a job.

B: What do you do?

A: I'm a cook.

Page 66

# Your Turn

**Refer to the general instructions on page x in the Introduction.**

## Preparation

With the class discuss the four jobs listed in Your Turn. What do people do in these jobs? Does anyone in the class have one of these jobs?

## Extension

 **Option:** In mixed-literacy level classes, you may want to give students additional practice with Book 1, Unit 2 Vocabulary Prompts page 12.

## Listening Script

A: I need a job.

B: What do you do?

A: I'm a cook.

B: Look. Here's an ad for a cook.

## Reading for Real

**Refer to the general instructions on page xii in the Introduction.**

## Exercise 3

### Preparation

1. As you read aloud each of the ads, have students look back at page 65 and find the pictures for the jobs.
2. Check comprehension by having students show the times on an analog clock and then calculate the number of hours a day for each of the jobs.
3. In addition, ask students to say or dial on a phone the number to call for each of the advertised jobs.

### Presentation

1. Tell students to circle the job titles and phone numbers in the ads and underline the times.
2. Encourage students to discuss their preferences for work times: mornings, afternoons, or evenings.

### Answers to Exercise 3

First ad: *Painter, 655-9275* should be circled; *8:00 A.M.–12:00 P.M.* should be underlined.

Second ad: *Dishwasher, 422-5533* should be circled; *5:00 P.M.–10:00 P.M.* should be underlined.

Third ad: *Driver, 479-8110* should be circled; *2:00 P.M.–6:00 P.M.*

## Page 67

## Exercise 4

**Refer to the general instructions on page xii in the Introduction.**

### Preparation

Elicit from students that the text on the right is from newspaper ads for these jobs.

### Presentation

Review each ad with the class. Answer any questions they have about vocabulary such as the following: *Opening, experience, line cook, busy, Delivery, record, immediate,* and *flexible.*

### Answers to Exercise 4

The following words should be circled:

1. painter    2. cashier    3. cook    4. driver    5. dishwasher

## Exercise 5

**Refer to the general instructions on page xii in the Introduction.**

### Preparation

Review each picture with the class and answer any questions students may have.

## Answers to Exercise 5

1. Third picture    2. Fourth picture    3. First picture    4. Second picture

## Your Turn

Refer to the general instructions on page x in the Introduction.

### Presentation

Tell students to use the pictures to help them fill out the sentences correctly.

### Answers to Your Turn

1. cashier    2. dishwasher    3. painter

## In Your Experience

Refer to the general instructions on page x in the Introduction.

### Preparation

1. Review personal information questions and sight words *name, address,* and *phone number.*
2. Practice questions and answers about occupations. Make sure students can identify their own occupations.
3. Help students write the names of their own jobs. You may want to have students draw a picture or cut out a picture of their own jobs and label it.
4. Introduce the sight word *job.* Hold up a word card and have students respond with the names of their jobs.

### Presentation

Ask students to answer the question and then to fill in the form. Go around the room helping as needed and checking students' work.

## Person to Person

Refer to the general instructions on page xii in the Introduction.

### Preparation

Generate a class list of jobs and write them on the board for students to refer to.

### Listening Script

A: What do you do?

B: I'm a driver. What do you do?

A: I'm a painter.

# Reading for Real

Refer to the general instructions on page xii in the Introduction.

## Preparation

1. Write the current year on the right side of the board. Model reading the year and have students repeat. If needed, use a calendar to help explain the year.

2. Draw a horizontal line across the board to create a time line. Mark and label other years on the time line. Say a year and ask a volunteer to point to it on the time line. Then point to a year and have students say the year.

3. Talk about your own past work. Use the time line to show the years. For example, say "I was a waiter from 1992 to 1995." Encourage volunteers to talk about their own work experience using the same format.

## Answers to Reading for Real

1. cashier
2. Mill Cafe

**Page 70**

# Sound Bites

Refer to the general instructions on page ix in the Introduction.

# Exercise 6

## Extension

 **Option:** In mixed-literacy level classes, you may want to give students additional practice with Book 1, Unit 4 Reading for Real page 15.

## Answers to Exercise 6

| | | | |
|---|---|---|---|
| 1. 1980 | 2. 1993 | 3. 1995 | 4. 1988 |
| 5. 1991 | 6. 1971 | 7. 1963 | 8. 1985 |

## Listening Script

1. Nineteen-eighty.
2. Nineteen ninety-three.
3. Nineteen ninety-five.
4. Nineteen eighty-eight.
5. Nineteen ninety-one.
6. Nineteen seventy-one.
7. Nineteen sixty-three.
8. Nineteen eighty-five.

# Exercise 7

Refer to the general instructions on page xii in the Introduction.

## Answers to Exercise 7

| | | |
|---|---|---|
| 1. 1973 | 2. 1998 | 3. 1991 |
| 4. 1987 | 5. 1974 | 6. 1980 |

## Listening Script

1. Nineteen seventy-three.
2. Nineteen ninety-eight.
3. Nineteen ninety-one.
4. Nineteen eighty-seven.
5. Nineteen seventy-four.
6. Nineteen eighty.

# Your Turn

Refer to the general instructions on page x in the Introduction.

## Preparation

Have students read the years. You might present résumés such as the simple ones found in more advanced levels of this program. You can put these on an overhead transparency and help students find the years. Then ask comprehension questions.

## Answers to Your Turn

The following information should be added to the job application:

Address: 317          Phone: 472-6632          Dates: 1993–1997

## Page 71

# Sound Bites

Refer to the general instructions on page ix in the Introduction.

# Exercise 8

## Preparation

Review the job application with the class. Point out where there are two phone numbers, two occupations, and two dates. Tell students to circle the one they hear.

## Answers to Exercise 8

The following information should be circled:

Phone: 437-6615          Job Titles: dishwasher, cook          Dates: 1990–1996

## Listening Script

A: Can I help you?

B: Yes. My name is Marc Sedar. I need a job.

A: OK. What's your phone number?

B: Four-three-seven, six-six-one-five.

A: Address?

B: 155 West Street. Somerville, Massachusetts.

A: What's your zip code?

B: Oh-two-one-one-five.

A: Do you work now?

B: Yes. I'm a dishwasher.

A: Where?

B: At the Mill Cafe.

A: What did you do before?

B: I was a cook in my country.

A: When?

B: From nineteen-ninety to nineteen ninety-six.

A: Where was that?

B: Amelia's Restaurant.

## Your Turn

Refer to the general instructions on page x in the Introduction.

### Presentation

1. Model the sample dialogue. Have students repeat each line.

2. Invite pairs of students to say the dialogue.

3. Write on the board column headings *Name* and *Job Title.*

4. Ask volunteers their names and jobs and demonstrate writing the information under the column headings. Remind students to ask for spellings and for repetitions as needed.

5. Invite a volunteer to ask the questions and record the information on the chart on the board.

### Extension

1. Tell students to interview three others in the class and record the information on a chart similar to the one on the board. Go around the room helping as needed.

2. Ask students to give the job titles of others in the class. Complete the chart on the board so students can check their work.

## Culture Corner

Refer to the general instructions on page xiii in the Introduction.

## Exercise 9

### Preparation

1. Make a list of jobs that students had in their native countries on the board.

2. Encourage students to discuss which of the jobs are found in the local area.

### Presentation

1. Make a chart on the board similar to the one on page 72. List jobs in the appropriate columns as students suggest them. Students can fill in jobs on the charts in their books.

2. Bring in pictures of other jobs and ask students if these jobs are common in their native countries and/or in the United States. Include these jobs on the chart.

3. Encourage students to discuss similarities and differences in jobs found in the United States and in their native countries.

### Extension

 **Option:** In mixed-literacy level classes, you may want to give students additional practice with Book 1, Unit 2 Vocabulary Prompts page 16.

### Answers to Exercise 9

Answers will vary.

# Exercise 10

**Refer to the general instructions on page xii in the Introduction.**

## Presentation

1. Bring in international warning or danger signs, including ones for no smoking, poison, high voltage, fire alarm, fire extinguisher. Discuss with the group where each of the signs is found and what the signs mean. Introduce gestures that are associated with warnings.

2. Write the words for each of the signs on cards. Make sure to use the words for the signs at the bottom of page 72.

3. Present the corresponding words and corresponding symbols at the bottom on page 72. Explain that they mean the same thing. Guide students to notice initial letters and the number of letters and words on the signs. Students do not need to read all of the words, but should be able to recognize from context that the words indicate danger.

4. If possible, go around the building looking for similar signs.

5. Tell students to notice if the signs studied are found in their workplaces or in other buildings they visit. Ask them to use the chart at the bottom of page 72 to report on the signs that they see. Encourage students to share with the class where they saw the signs.

## Extension

1. Students can write questions (or just the question words) on a set of cards. Here are some examples:

    - What (do you do)?
    - When (were you a ___)?
    - Where (were you a ___)?

    Students can write their responses on another set of cards. Tell students to practice matching the questions and answers. As an alternative, have students write the sight words on a set of cards: *job title, dates, employer*. Students can match the sight words with the responses.

2. Bring in examples of job applications. Have students find the sections that ask about work history. If possible, make copies of the applications and have students practice filling in their work experience.

3. Ask students to find job titles in newspaper want ads. Make a list of specific job titles for students to look for and circle. Students can discuss times and phone numbers that are also found in the ads.

4. Introduce and practice the suffix *-er*. Point out that it is commonly found in job titles. Ask students to look back through the unit for jobs that end with *-er*. Students can suggest other jobs that they may know with the same ending such as the following: *farmer, teacher, helper, worker, assembler.*

## Answers to Exercise 10

NO SMOKING: c

FLAMMABLE: b

POISON: a

HIGH VOLTAGE: d

FIRE EXTINGUISHER: e

## OVERVIEW

### Objectives

#### Skills and Structures

Demonstrate understanding of money terms and amounts

Ask and answer simple questions about prices

Recognize prices on advertisements

Write money amounts

Add and subtract money to determine total price and change

Recognize payment options (cash, credit, check)

#### SCANS Competencies

Foundation Skills

#### Realia

Authentic coins or play money

Retail flyers

Price tags

Canceled checks

Credit cards

## ACTIVITY NOTES

### Page 73

### Spotlight

**Refer to the general instructions on page xi in the Introduction.**

NOTE: The names of the coins are not taught in this lesson. Focus on just the value of the coins.

#### Preparation

There are various ways for saying money amounts. For example: $1.80 = *one dollar and eighty cents, a dollar eighty,* or *one eighty.* You may want to expose students to the variety of ways prices are read, but have students practice saying just one form.

## Sound Bites

Refer to the general instructions on page ix in the Introduction.

## Exercise 1

### Listening Script

| | |
|---|---|
| One cent. | One dollar. |
| Five cents. | Five dollars. |
| Ten cents. | Ten dollars. |
| Twenty-five cents. | Twenty dollars. |

## Exercise 2

Refer to the general instructions on page xii in the Introduction.

### Presentation

Play or read the whole dialogue for students. Then play or read each line and have students repeat it individually and as a class.

### Listening Script

A: How much is this?

B: It's seventy-five cents.

**Page 74**

## Your Turn

Refer to the general instructions on page x in the Introduction.

### Preparation

1. Review or present the names of the items used in Your Turn.
2. Model the pronunciation of the prices in Your Turn. Have students repeat.

### Listening Script

A: How much is this?

B: It's seventy-five cents.

A: Thanks.

B: You're welcome.

## Reading for Real

Refer to the general instructions on page xii in the Introduction.

## Presentation

1. Read aloud the prices on the flyer on page 74. Ask students to circle them as you read.

2. Point to an item in the exercise and ask, "How much is this?" Invite a volunteer to read the price.

3. Arrange students in pairs and have them practice asking and answering questions about the price of the items.

4. Invite pairs to present their exchanges to the class.

### Page 75

# Exercise 3

**Refer to the general instructions on page xii in the Introduction.**

## Preparation

Before doing these exercises, ask students to say money amounts as you indicate different groupings of coins and bills. Then write amounts on the board and ask students to find combinations of coins and bills to equal the amounts.

## Answers to Exercise 3

1. $1.25      2. $2.40      3. $5.25      4. $3.15      5. $10.50

# Exercise 4

**Refer to the general instructions on page xii in the Introduction.**

## Answers to Exercise 4

1. Illustration showing $5 bill, 3 quarters
2. Illustration showing 3 dollar bills, 2 quarters, 1 dime, 1 nickel
3. Illustration showing $1 bill, 1 quarter, 1 dime
4. Illustration showing 2 dollar bills, 4 dimes
5. Illustration showing $10 bill, 2 dollar bills, 2 quarters

### Page 76

# Your Turn

**Refer to the general instructions on page x in the Introduction.**

# Exercise 5

## Answers to Exercise 5

1. $6.75      2. $11.15      3. $6.85      4. $15.50

# Exercise 6

**Refer to the general instructions on page xii in the Introduction.**

## Presentation

Have students practice adding and subtracting with real or play money. Students do not need to read the equations, but they should be able to say the answers to the problems.

## Answers to Exercise 6

1. 75¢     2. 85¢     3. $5.00     4. $4.55

5. 75¢     6. 50¢     7. $1.25     8. $3.50

**Page 77**

# Person to Person

Refer to the general instructions on page xii in the Introduction.

## Preparation

Point out that the price tags tell how much something is. The money underneath each tag is the amount students have to spend. Ask students how much change they will receive for each item.

## Presentation

You may want to have the class use money (real or play) to act out the dialogue.

**Option:** If students are advanced, you may want to have them discuss and role-play how to disagree when the change is incorrect.

## Listening Script

A: How much is it?

B: That's three dollars.

A: Here's five dollars.

B: Two dollars is your change.

A: Thank you.

# Reading for Real

Refer to the general instructions on page xii in the Introduction.

## Presentation

It is not necessary to teach the usage of *is/are* for students to complete the exercise. If students ask, point out that *is* is used with singular subjects and *are* with plural subjects.

## Answers to Reading for Real

1. $1.25     2. $1.75     3. $2.18

4. $2.00     5. $5.14

**Page 78**

# Sound Bites

Refer to the general instructions on page ix in the Introduction.

# Exercise 7

## Answers to Exercise 7

1. $3.80     2. $10.75     3. $9.25     4. $3.92

5. $11.40     6. $23.79     7. $18.10     8. $15.60

### Listening Script

1. It's three eighty.
2. That costs ten seventy-five.
3. That's nine twenty-five.
4. It's three ninety-two.
5. That costs eleven forty.
6. That's twenty-three seventy-nine.
7. It's eighteen ten.
8. That costs fifteen sixty.

## Exercise 8

Refer to the general instructions on page xii in the Introduction.

### Preparation

Write a list of classroom objects on the board. Have students ask you how much the classroom objects cost. While you tell them the answer, have a volunteer write the price on the board next to the item.

### Answers to Exercise 8

1. $7.33    2. $20.85    3. $9.10    4. $15.55    5. $4.99    6. $30.72

### Listening Script

1. Seven dollars and thirty-three cents.
2. Twenty dollars and eighty-five cents.
3. Nine dollars and ten cents.
4. Fifteen dollars and fifty-five cents.
5. Four dollars and ninety-nine cents.
6. Thirty dollars and seventy-two cents.

## In Your Experience

Refer to the general instructions on page x in the Introduction.

### Preparation

1. If there are vending machines in the building, have the class go to them and read the prices for items. Alternatively, bring in common items with price tags and have students practice reading the prices.

### Presentation

1. Students can work in pairs or small groups writing the prices. Have them use information they know from their experience to answer. Point out that prices can vary.
2. Have students share their responses. Compare the answers and discuss differences in prices of some items.

### Answers to In Your Experience

Prices will vary.

1. bus ticket: $1.00    2. telephone call: 35¢    3. stamp: 32¢    4. pop (soda): 50¢
5. coffee: 50¢

### Page 79

## Person to Person

Refer to the general instructions on page xii in the Introduction.

### Presentation

1. Model the sample dialogue. Have students repeat each line.
2. Invite pairs of students to present the dialogue.

## Listening Script

A: How much is it?

B: It's two seventy-five.

## Pages 79-80

# Your Turn

**Refer to the general instructions on page x in the Introduction.**

## Presentation

1. Arrange students into groups A and B.

2. Tell Group A to look at the store flyer on page 79. Have them find the prices and notice which prices are missing. Explain that they will ask questions to find out the missing prices.

3. Tell Group B to look at the flyer on page 80. Help them read the prices. Explain that they will give the prices to their partners.

4. Pair students from A with students from B. A will ask questions and B will respond. A will fill in the missing prices on the flyer.

5. Then have B ask questions and A respond with the prices.

6. Tell students to check the prices with their partners.

7. Invite pairs to present the questions and answers to the class.

## Answers to Your Turn

| *Student A* | *Student B* |
|---|---|
| Envelopes $1.75 | Pencil: 39¢ |
| Notebook: $1.19 | Scissors: $2.25 |
| Pen: 49¢ | Marker: $1.65 |
| Stapler: $3.45 | Paper: 79¢ |

## Page 80

# Culture Corner

**Refer to the general instructions on page xiii in the Introduction.**

## Preparation

Bring in examples of checks and charge or credit cards. Encourage students to share what they know about these forms of payment. Introduce vocabulary *cash, charge, check.*

## Presentation

1. Have students look at the material on page 80. Ask students to point to the forms of payment as you say them.

2. Model the statement and question of the salesclerk. Have students respond with the different forms of payment.

3. Explain that all stores accept cash, but not all stores accept checks and charge or credit cards. Discuss other information or documents that might be requested when paying by check or charge/credit cards such as driver's license, photo ID.

## Extension

1. Give students a list of items (or illustrations of items) and have them go to different stores to record prices. When students return, compare the prices. Encourage students to talk about the stores they usually go to and why they like these stores.

2. Set up a store in the classroom. Students can make price tags for classroom items and make displays. Have one student play the role of a salesclerk. Tell others students to go to the store to buy items. The salesclerk can total the items and make change. Encourage students to use the dialogues from the unit as they role-play.

3. Depending on the level of the students, practice *How much is/are . . . ? It is/They are . . . .* Make a chart of singular and plural items. Explain that is is used with singular items and are is used with plural items. Have students ask and answer questions about the price of the items on the chart.

4. Review and practice consonant digraphs *ch, th,* and *sh.* Model the sounds and practice them in words from this unit: *ch (much, charge, check ); th (thank, this, that); sh (cash).*

**Option:** In mixed-literacy level classes, you may want to give students additional practice with Book 1, Unit 7 Culture Corner page 66.

# UNIT 9                                    LET'S EAT

## OVERVIEW

### Objectives

#### Skills and Structures

Demonstrate understanding of common food names

Express basic needs with simple phrases

Demonstrate understanding of prices and quantities

Ask and answer simple questions about location of items in a store

Read prices from a store flyer

Ask and answer questions about price

Write money amounts

Demonstrate understanding of coupons

#### SCANS Competencies

Foundation Skills

#### Realia

Newspaper food ads

Supermarket flyers

Coupons for food

# ACTIVITY NOTES

Page 81

## Spotlight

Refer to the general instructions on page xi in the Introduction.

### Preparation

Introduce and practice the names of food items that students use in the exercises.

## Sound Bites

Refer to the general instructions on page ix in the Introduction.

## Exercise 1

### Presentation

Tell students they will hear the names of all the foods in the picture.

### Listening Script

1. Apples.
2. Oranges.
3. Lettuce.
4. Tomatoes.
5. Fish.
6. Chicken.
7. Meat.

## Exercise 2

Refer to the general instructions on page xii in the Introduction.

### Presentation

Play or read the whole dialogue for students. Then play or read each line and have students repeat it individually and as a class.

### Listening Script

A: I need fish.

B: It's in aisle three.

Page 82

## Your Turn

Refer to the general instructions on page x in the Introduction.

### Presentation

Remind students to use the information in the picture in the dialogues.

### Listening Script

A: I need apples.

B: They're in aisle one.

A: Thanks.

# Reading for Real

Refer to the general instructions on page xii in the Introduction.

### Presentation

1. Ask students to identify the food items in the illustration.
2. Say the prices and have students point to them.
3. Read aloud the price labels for the food items. Introduce the quantity terms and abbreviated forms as needed: *bag, pound (lb.), dozen (doz.), loaf,* and *head.*
4. Say the names of food items and have volunteers read the prices aloud.
5. If possible, bring in food containers and price labels. Students can find the prices and quantity terms on the labels.

## Page 83

# Exercise 3

Refer to the general instructions on page xii in the Introduction.

### Extension

 **Option:** In mixed-literacy level classes, you may want to give students additional practice with Book 1, Unit 5, Vocabulary Prompts, pages 42 and 47.

### Answers to Exercise 3

1. eggs
2. bananas
3. fish
4. rice
5. chicken

# Exercise 4

Refer to the general instructions on page xii in the Introduction.

### Answers to Exercise 4

1. AISLE 1
2. AISLE 2
3. AISLE 3
4. AISLE 2
5. AISLE 1

## Page 84

# Your Turn

Refer to the general instructions on page x in the Introduction.

### Preparation

With the class review the price tags and answer any questions students may have about vocabulary such as the following: *bag, lb. (pound), head, doz. (dozen),* and *loaf.*

## Answers to Your Turn

1. $2.49      2. 85¢      3. $1.19/doz.      4. $3.75/lb.

5. 75¢      6. $3.25      7. 69¢      8. 49¢

# Person to Person

**Refer to the general instructions on page xii in the Introduction.**

## Preparation

1. Ask questions about prices of the items in the exercise at the top of the page. As you ask, write the food items on the board to create the following two-column chart:

| | |
|---|---|
| bread | oranges |
| fish | eggs |
| lettuce | tomatoes |
| rice | bananas |

2. Point to *bread* in the first column and say, "How much is the bread?" Have students repeat the question. Then point to the next item and invite a volunteer to ask a question. Continue with the other items in the first column.

3. Point to *oranges* in the second column and say, "How much are the oranges?" Have the class repeat. Encourage students to create questions with the other items in the second column.

4. Write "How much is . . . ?" and "How much are . . . ?" as column headings for the chart. Invite students to suggest differences they see between the questions. You may want to point out the -*s* at the end of the items in the second column. Explain that *is* is used with the first column and *are* is used with the second column.

## Listening Script

A: How much is the fish?

B: Three-fifty a pound.

A: How much are the eggs?

B: A dollar nineteen.

## Page 85

# Reading for Real

**Refer to the general instructions on page xii in the Introduction.**

## Presentation

Elicit from or remind students that *per pound* is often written as /*lb.*

## Answers to Reading for Real

1. $2.85/lb.      2. $65¢/lb.      3. 75¢/lb.      4. $2.00/lb.

5. 99¢      6. $1.99      7. $2.49/lb.

# Sound Bites

Refer to the general instructions on page ix in the Introduction.

# Exercise 5

## Presentation

Remind students to listen for the whole price, not just the first numbers.

## Answers to Exercise 5

| | | | |
|---|---|---|---|
| 1. 79¢ | 2. $1.15 | 3. 27¢ | 4. $3.39 |
| 5. $1.48 | 6. $2.99 | 7. 55¢ | 8. $4.09 |

## Listening Script

1. The bread is seventy-nine cents.
2. The eggs are a dollar fifteen a dozen.
3. The apple is twenty-seven cents.
4. The fish is three dollars and thirty-nine cents a pound.
5. The bag costs a dollar forty-eight.
6. Oranges cost two dollars and ninety-nine cents a bag.
7. The bananas are fifty-five cents a pound.
8. This meat is four dollars and nine cents a pound.

# Exercise 6

Refer to the general instructions on page xii in the Introduction.

## Presentation

Remind students to write in the dollar sign and period or the cent sign when they are writing the prices.

## Answers to Exercise 6

| | | |
|---|---|---|
| 1. 45¢ | 2. 82¢ | 3. 37¢ |
| 4. $4.86 | 5. $1.25 | 6. $2.98 |

## Listening Script

1. It's on sale for forty-five cents.
2. That box costs eighty-two cents.
3. This can is thirty-seven cents.
4. The chicken costs four dollars and eighty-six cents.
5. The tomatoes are one dollar and twenty-five cents a pound.
6. The bag of rice costs two dollars and ninety-eight cents.

# In Your Experience

Refer to the general instructions on page x in the Introduction.

## Presentation

Have students look for actual prices in supermarket flyers or in supermarkets to complete the activity.

## Answers to In Your Experience

Answers will vary.

# Person to Person

Refer to the general instructions on page xii in the Introduction.

## Presentation

Tell students to use the price information in the supermarket flyer on page 87 to ask and answer the questions.

## Listening Script

A: How much are the eggs?

B: One-oh-nine.

# Your Turn

Refer to the general instructions on page x in the Introduction.

## Preparation

1. Model the sample dialogue. Have students repeat after you.
2. Arrange students into groups A and B.
3. Tell Group A to look at the store flyer on page 87. Have them find the prices and notice which prices are missing. Explain that they will ask questions to find out the missing prices. Remind students of the two forms *How much is . . . ?* and *How much are . . . ?* Tell students to decide which question form to use for each of the blank items.
4. Tell Group B to look at the flyer on page 88. Repeat the above procedure.

## Presentation

1. Pair students from A with students from B. A will ask questions and B will give prices. A will fill in the missing prices on the flyer.
2. Then have B ask questions and A respond with the prices.
3. Tell students to check the prices with their partners.
4. Invite pairs to present the questions and answers to the class.

## Answers to Your Turn

*Student A*

Tomatoes: 95¢

Lettuce: $1.15

Rice: $4.80

Bananas: 39¢

*Student B*

Eggs: $1.09

Bread: 65¢

Apples: $1.89

Oranges: $2.49

Fish: $3.25

Page 88

# Culture Corner

**Refer to the general instructions on page xiii in the Introduction.**

## Preparation

1. Bring in examples of coupons. Encourage students to share what they know about coupons.

2. Tell students to find the coupons on page 88. Ask students to read the money amounts and names of food items on the coupons. Guide students to discover if the money is the price or money should be subtracted from the price. Point out words such as the following: *Off*, and *2 for.*

3. Have students calculate the price of various items if a coupon is 25¢ off or 50¢ off. For example, say "Apples are $1.99 a bag. I have a coupon for 25¢ off. How much are the apples?" Ask questions with *2 for* . . . . For example, say "Lettuce is 59¢. How much are 2 heads of lettuce? I have a coupon for lettuce: 2 for $1. How much money do I save?"

4. Students can look through local newspapers or store flyers for coupons. Encourage students to comment on which coupons they might use and which they might not use. Ask them to explain why.

## Extension

1. Bring in flyers from local supermarkets. Have students look through and compare prices of various items. Students can talk about where they go to buy food.

2. Students can prepare shopping lists. Have students check flyers or go to stores to find the prices of the items on their lists. Students can total the amounts of the items.

3. As a group, discuss ways to save money when shopping. Discuss using coupons, buying in bulk, comparing unit prices, noting sales, and buying in-season produce.

4. If students are interested, compare metric measurements and standard measurements for weight: kilograms/pounds. Help students find metric measurements on boxes and labels.

5. Introduce and practice the long vowel sound often written with *ee, ea.* Model the sound and practice with words from the unit: *need, meat, eat, repeat, read,* and *three.* Other common words to practice are these: *see, keep, seat, bean, feed, tea, feel,* and *real.*